Rehound 1984

New Dawn in Japan

Everett F. Briggs

LONGMANS, GREEN & COMPANY

TORONTO   NEW YORK

Cum Permissu Superiorum

Nihil obstat: JOHN M. A. FEARNS, S.T.D., *Censor of books*

Imprimatur: FRANCIS CARDINAL SPELLMAN, *Archbishop of New York*

September 14, 1948

Contents

1. The Light That Failed

THE DEFEAT OF JAPAN was, in the eyes of the hitherto-undefeated descendants of the samurai, a catastrophe little short of the end of the world. True, the Japanese people had not been stunned by a single, sudden blow from the mailed fist of Mars. They had had ample time to anticipate the tidal wave of desolation that was destined finally to engulf them. Had not their censored press carried accounts of all the battles in the South Pacific—battles that usually attended "enemy attempts at landing?" All these attempts, of course, had been described as ending in failure.

Despite the feigned optimism of the controlled press, however, it began to occur to many intelligent Japanese that those monumental "failures" of the American Army and Navy were marching steadily northwards, straight to the portals of Nippon. Finally, came the great "failure" at Saipan—a failure much too close at hand to be distorted into a Japanese victory. The secret was out. The war was lost! Indeed, it had been lost with the recapture of the Philippines, as Premier Koiso had forewarned. But the people had clung to the slim hope of some face-saving settlement short of utter defeat, until first Saipan, and then Iwo Jima, fell to the victorious forces of the United States.

In the bombbursts of those defeats, the Japanese clearly beheld the stark realities of the situation: the promised victory, the assured prestige of empire, the rivers of milk and honey—all were but the cruelest of mirages. The Japanese realized at last to what extent they had been the gullible victims of the mendacious propaganda of their own stupid and dictatorial government. The issue was no longer in doubt. The proverbial jig was up. The Japanese people knew it. The Japanese Government knew it. And the government knew that the people knew it.

Still, to quote Father Patrick J. Byrne—a Maryknoll missioner who was interned in Japan throughout the war—that little gang of fanatical diehards, "rather than admit defeat, was quite willing to see the whole nation reduced to bones and ashes."

We can well imagine the black despair of those poor people, whom a dictatorship reserved like sheep for slaughter, as they huddled in their little bamboo huts, awaiting the foreign fury from the skies. The Japanese people were well aware, as Father Byrne declared, that they had no one to blame for their wretched plight except their own callous government. Thus, their contempt and hatred for their leaders mounted in proportion to their own terror and despair, so that their reaction to the twin tragedies of the atomic bombings early in August, 1945, was mainly one of relief rather than resentment. Resentment there was, of course; but it was directed not so much against the United States as against their own government, which had obliged the B-29's to wreak such havoc long after the war had been lost.

After the "sheet of sun" had flashed across the cities of Hiroshima and Nagasaki, in that first dawn of the cosmic age, the Japanese found their homeland desolated beyond description. Far worse than the desolation, however, was the impenetrable gloom that ensued upon those two prodigious gleams of awful glory. The lamp in the soul of Japan had flickered and gone out. For a long time, its flame had been fanned by the lies and false hopes of official propaganda. But now, in the dawn of the atomic age, the Japanese people saw the truth, and the gust of its approach extinguished the poor candles of myth, propaganda, and wishful thinking, which had burned feebly amid the twilight obsequies of a semi-feudal state.

The rising sun of the Japanese had set. The very props of their national consciousness had been shaken. All their historic aspirations, their corporate convictions, their social and emotional values—in fact, the whole fabric of their psychological legacy—seemed utterly to disintegrate amid the rude revelations of that cosmic dawn, when Japan first beheld her face as others long before had seen it. As the potsherds of her national sanctities lay strewn around her, Japan's disillusionment was complete.

This ideological vacuum in the soul of Japan is probably the keenest hurt of her defeat. The Japanese people, religious at heart, feel the need of new spiritual values to replace those that they have lost. Their indigenous religions, both Shinto and Buddhism, which after all are codes of individual rather than social conduct, have failed them.

Shinto—the "Way of the Gods"—hardly is entitled to be called a religion. Originally, it was nothing more than animism, which found its outward expression in nature worship. Doctor Masaharu Anesaki, a Japanese authority on the subject, states: "Natural objects which evoked a thrill of emotion, whether affectionate or awe-inspiring, were regarded as *kami,* or superior ones." If these natural objects themselves were not elevated to the rank of divinities, at least they were presumed to be the favored dwelling-places of the spirits that inform the world of nature. Thus terrible thunder, lightning, fire, and earthquake; milder wind and rain; zephyrs on a mountain top, cascades in a forest's gloom, a gnarled pine to rheumatism long resigned—all these things, according to the cult of Shinto, may enshrine their separate deities.

Although the *kami* of nature were innumerable, they were not numerous enough for a Japanese pantheon. So as time went on, the departed ancestors of the race were deified: first, the forebears of individual families; then the souls of deceased communal chieftains; and finally the ancestors of the ruling clan. To pay due homage to these myriad *kami* at the family shrine, the village shrine, or the imperial sanctuary, as the case might be, was the essence of primitive Shinto.

There was not the least systematization of these simple notions affecting the divinities of Shinto. Therefore, no organized body of doctrine, no canon of sacred books, existed. Moreover, there was not the slightest ethical complexion to the practical features of this primitive quasi-religion. In short, the "Way of the Gods" originally was not, and never afterwards became, a religion in the strict ethical sense of the word. Once the nature spirits had been amalgamated with the souls of deceased ancestors, Shinto became essentially little more than a reverential attitude adopted by the Japanese toward their departed forbears.

Shinto, then, might be defined as the elemental religion of a warrior race, which was well satisfied with its one tenet of loyalty. That single word summed up the whole moral content of ancient Shinto: loyalty to the gods, commensurate with their rank in the celestial hierarchy, and proportionate loyalty to their descendants here on earth. It was in this quasi-religious soil, fertilized at once by superstition and human ambition, that the supposed "divinity" of the Japanese emperors began to germinate.

Inasmuch as the greatest of the great were the ancestors of the Yamato clan, their descendants in turn

were entitled to a place of primacy among the govern-
ing classes. In this way Shinto became associated
intimately with the ruling family. It was the power
behind the throne, inspiring patriotism while reinforc-
ing reverence for the Emperor. On the other hand, the
throne became the champion and mainstay of Shinto,
employing it to emphasize the "divine" origin and exalt
the temporal power of the "Son of Heaven."

In the middle of the sixth century, however, Shinto
suffered a distinct setback, as a result of the importation
of the "Law of Buddha." Buddhism, already a thousand
years old in India, entered Japan by way of Korea,
whither it had gone from China. Hyakusai, ruler of one
of Korea's three feudal states, is said to have sent a
golden image of Buddha to the Emperor Kimmei, in
A.D. 552. Because of the predominance of Shinto at
the court, the idol suffered many vicissitudes; but finally it was enshrined in a private home, which became
the first Buddhist temple in Japan. Subsequently, monks
and nuns flocked in from Korea, and the new religion
began to make slow but steady progress in Japan, especially among the upper classes. During the reign of
Shotoku (A.D. 593-621), Buddhism became the established religion, although Shinto was not in any way
suppressed. From that time onwards, the "Law of Buddha" was recognized as the greatest civilizing agency
in Japan. Every walk of life was better for the influence
of the Sage of India.

Shinto had never had much genuine religious appeal for the Japanese people. It was powerless to resist the allure of Buddhism, which offered profound metaphysics, a lofty moral code, and solemn ritual. When, therefore, Kobo Daishi (A.D. 774-835), one of Japan's most famous ecclesiastics, diplomatically identified the *kami* of Shinto as reincarnations of the Buddhist saints and divinities, the conquest of the primitive religion was complete.

Basil Hall Chamberlain, a noted authority on Japanese antiquities, remarks, "Buddhism was the teacher under whose instruction the Japanese nation grew up." In the course of centuries, its influence subtly pervaded every sphere of Japan's national life—education, social uplift, and cultural aspiration of every kind.

Still Shinto was not entirely displaced, much less suppressed. The hold of the *kami* on the popular imagination was too strong to be easily disengaged immediately. The religion of the Japanese people at this time might be described as a kind of dualism, in which the "Law of Buddha" had attained to a position of equality with the "Way of the Gods." This compound of Shintoism and Buddhism received the name of *Ryobu Shinto,* meaning "Two-department Shinto," because the rites of both religions often were performed in the same building. Most Shinto shrines, according to Doctor Anesaki, were furnished with "inner sanctuaries" where the Buddhist ceremonial might be performed. For the new religion, however, more conspicuous successes lay ahead.

In the latter half of the twelfth century, at the beginning of the Kamakura period (A.D. 1185-1308), Honen, one of Japan's great spiritual leaders, appeared on the scene. The fundamental tenet of his teaching was universal redemption through the mercy of all-compassionate Buddha in the person of Amida, "Lord of the Western Paradise." Good works, said Honen, are unnecessary. Faith alone suffices for salvation. It is enough to invoke the Buddha in testimony of one's faith, under the saving formula: "*Namu Amida Butsu*" —"Adoration to the Buddha of Infinite Life and Light!"

Honen's appearance could not have been more timely. The common people of Japan were wretched and demoralized after thirty years of civil war between the powerful Taira and Minamoto clans. Honen's optimistic doctrine of unconditional salvation stirred new hopes in the hearts of a discouraged nation. In every corner of the land, the balm of this new brand of Buddhism was received enthusiastically; and in the intensity of that nation-wide welcome, Shinto retreated farther into the background. In the same century, Honen was followed by Shinran, another great Buddhist figure who preached universal salvation through faith alone. In Shinran's teaching there was no need of good works, since the well-intentioned man is predestined to the "timeless bliss" of the "pure land."

The pietistic teachings of Honen and Shinran were most consoling to the simple-minded majority of the nation. But the warrior class derived little satisfaction from such sentimental considerations. The swashbuckling samurai desired something more dynamic and invigorating. This, Buddhism offered them in the teachings of Zen.

Zen is really a method of spiritual development, which starts with concentration, and progresses through meditation to the goal of contemplation. According to Zen, man should not put his trust in prayers and creeds, but should seek ultimate reality in his own soul through the exercise of discipline and rigid self-control. Although this stern doctrine of spiritual development appealed chiefly to the samurai class, it gradually insinuated itself into the lives of the common people, by many of whom it was well received as an antidote to the emotionalism of other forms of Buddhism. Largely because of Zen's emphasis on mind training, the monks of this denomination became the educators of feudal Japan. In all their monasteries, they inaugurated *terakoya* or "temple schools," through the instrumentality of which the monks of Zen diffused knowledge and culture throughout the land.

With the downfall of the shogunate, in 1868, and the restoration of the Emperor to *de facto* sovereignty after an eclipse of almost seven hundred years, Shinto came into its own again. But lacking genuine religious sentiment, this severe cult of empty sanctuaries could not maintain its hold on the hearts of the Japanese people, and Buddhism soon rallied. Shinto, however, was destined to play the last act in the religious pageant of old Japan, when the impetuous descendants of the southern samurai clans of Satsuma and Choshu returned to power, following the reverses of the war with China in 1894-95.

But Shinto's little act soon vanished from the stage. The end of World War II spelled finis for this simple creed of quasi-religious loyalty, which had been prostituted by the military to serve their own ambitious ends. Early in 1946, Emperor Hirohito, whose very name was a forbidden word, in a startling self-repudiation called a halt to the nonsense that the militaristic psychopaths had tried so long to foist upon the Japanese people. The Emperor stated very simply that his relation to the people of Japan was founded on affection rather than myth. He denied his own "divinity," and renounced forever Japan's much-vaunted "divine" mission to rule the world—a mission, incidentally, that was not of his own devising.

Indeed, the Emperor had had abundant reason to suspect his alleged divinity. If there is any prerogative to which deity must lay claim, it is the right to be accorded the independence of action conceded to the average business man. In fact, however, Emperor Hirohito was little more than putty in the hands of the military, despite their outward show of respect in his presence and the din that they raised in public over his official divinity. On occasion, the Emperor apparently found it difficult to conceal his disgust at this hypocrisy of which he was the victim. For this surmise we have only a cryptic remark made by the late Admiral Shinjiro Yamamoto, Japan's most outstanding Catholic in recent times; but this remark, coupled with our knowledge of the Emperor's education and travels, is sufficient ground for the assertion that Emperor Hirohito never believed the myth of his divinity.

Admiral Yamamoto—not to be confused with the man who aspired to dictate the "peace" terms in the White House—resigned from the Imperial Japanese Navy, because as a captain he was required to officiate at Shinto ceremonies aboard ship. The reason for his resignation was well known in high government circles. The admiral's sterling character won the respect of the imperial family, and three times he was requested to act as tutor for the Crown Prince, who is now Emperor Hirohito.

It was this brave Christian gentleman, so intimate with the Emperor, who is reported to have said, "If you only knew what His Majesty thinks of his divinity!"

Nevertheless, the imperial renunciation of "divinity" was an atom bomb no less cataclysmic in the world of Japanese thought than the bombs that had fallen on the cities of Hiroshima and Nagasaki. The fantastic universe in which the Japanese people had been dwelling collapsed about them like a house of cards. Then they realized for the first time that, whereas they were materially, industrially, culturally, and politically a world power, they were spiritually, psychologically, emotionally, and religiously living in an age of myth. They understood for the first time the enigma they had presented to the eyes of foreigners, who had been amazed to hear Westernized people in modernized Tokyo seriously discussing the ancient gods and goddesses of mythology, which the Greeks and Romans had discarded some two thousand years ago.

Following the demise of state Shinto, Buddhism remained Christianity's only apparent competitor in the field of religion, until the passage of the recent law exempting shrines and temples from government control. Now, without the discipline imposed by law, Buddhism is deteriorating rapidly; there is scarcely one of its sects that has not been touched by schism and defection. Although the process of deterioration has not been as marked in Buddhism as in Shinto, which already has proliferated until there are now approximately eight hundred new sects, it is serious enough. The four leading Buddhist denominations—Jodo, Tendai, Shingon, and Nichiren—are rent with schism. Thirteen temples in Kyoto alone have seceded from the Jodo sect.

Various reasons may be alleged for these secessions, but the principal ones appear to be the following five:

First, the desire to re-establish the pre-war organization, in which the leading denominations were autonomous; second, a preference for independence, especially financial independence; third, such factors as prestige, jealousy, unwillingness to share expenses; fourth, dissatisfaction of the young bonzes with the doddering leadership, or lack of leadership, of older superiors; fifth, doctrinal cleavages, of which there is a plethora. Principally because of this deterioration, many of the Japanese people are losing confidence in Buddhism. In an hour of universal flux, it is unable to offer them stability or security.

With their religious faith, like their national faith, demoralized, the people naturally reach out to the only religion that appears to afford them a secure haven from the prevailing uncertainty. When the Japanese behold the sight of American GI's crowding their churches, they feel inwardly betrayed, because Buddhism seems to have denied to them what Christianity has bestowed upon those hardy warriors from across the seas. There are Japanese, the missioners say, who actually go to Catholic churches just to behold the look of peace upon the faces of our soldiers as they return from the Communion rail.

When the Japanese, going a step farther, investigate the tenets of the Christian religion, they are struck by the fact that Buddhism is much less dynamic than Christianity, and therefore is proportionately unsuited to the exigencies of the times in which they live. Buddhism speaks of rest—of rest, in a world that knows no rest—whereas, Christianity is eloquent of, and vibrant with, activity. True, both religions promise rest in the hereafter. But in the rest offered by Buddhism, the passionless repose of nirvana, there is more than a suspicion of annihilation; while the rest that Christianity holds out is active repose, or reposeful activity, like the tireless play of children in the morning sunlight. The latter concept of eternal rest is more adapted, and has a more natural appeal, to the genius of an indefatigable race.

Logically, too, Christianity is far more satisfying to thoughtful Japanese than is Buddhism. In the teaching of the Sage of India, for example, there is no Creator, but only an eternal spirit from which emanated the primal atoms, from which, in turn, all else originated by fortuitous combinations.

The author once asked an educated Japanese gentleman, a graduate of the Imperial University, what, in his opinion, was the root notion of Buddhism. He replied that it was the idea of "a wheel revolving in a field"— the wheel of endless mutation in the field of life. When the gentleman was asked if the motion of the wheel did not present a philosophical difficulty, he answered that it did not.

"But doesn't the transition from inertia to movement suggest a problem?"

"Now that you mention it," he admitted, "it does."

This, perhaps, is a fair appraisal of the situation: Christianity propounds difficulties, for the solution of which the Japanese mind can turn to Christianity alone.

Finally, the Christian religion is infinitely more hopeful than Buddhism, which is decidedly somber. According to Buddhism, misery is the essence of all life. To attain to nirvana is to be released from the merciless necessity of innumerable reincarnations in this vale of tears. But nirvana offers only cheerless release from worldly cares, in a state of absorption into the "world soul" in which, although individuality may cease, individual consciousness remains latent. In other words, nirvana is a state of life-in-death, or death-in-life, for which English has no word; that is, an immortality of subconsciousness reached only after pilgrimage through cycles of regret, the number of which no man knows, because "the eternal ages are long."

Out of sheer desperation, then, if from no worthier motive, the people of Japan are turning from Shinto and Buddhism to Christianity. The Christian religion, to be sure, is no stranger in their homeland. In the person of the Catholic Church, Christianity has become a part of Nippon's national heritage.

The history of the Catholic Church in Japan has been contemporaneous with the age of the samurai, the last vestiges of which have disappeared in the wake of World War II. It is perhaps with a little smart of nostalgia that many Japanese are being attracted to the

2. The Tale of Tenshu

IT HAPPENED a long time ago in Kagoshima, the principal city of Satsuma, which was the southernmost province in feudal Japan. The occasion was Our Lady's day—August 15, 1549. The inhabitants of Kagoshima, the gateway to Japan, had turned aside from the drab pursuits of everyday life to the colorful solemnities of *Bon*, the ancient festival of the dead.

With all the tenderness of their Buddhist faith, those Oriental people had vied with one another during three days, in comforting the spirits of their departed ancestors. In lowly homes and great, they bowed before the black, lacquered, funeral tablets inscribed with the names of dear ones whom they could never forget; they touched to their foreheads, in token of profound respect, the ritualistic offerings of choicest food and drink. In the dim vastnesses of lordly temples, faintly sweet with the smell of balsam, shaven bonzes knelt before their idols of Buddha, chanting the ancient sutras for all who had crossed the ocean of existence to the shores of nirvana-land. Kagoshima, like every other city in Japan, resounded with the muffled roll of temple drums, delicately punctuated by the silvery tinkling of sanctuary bells.

At the height of this moving ceremonial on the

Japanese equivalent of All Souls' Day, in the home of a samurai named Anjiro, a disconsolate little group sat bowed before the family shrine, in memory of their missing master. Three years earlier, he had fled for his life, aboard a foreign vessel, to the land of the "southern barbarians." In due time the "barbarian ship" had returned to Kagoshima, but of Anjiro and his manservant there had been no trace.

So, on that high festival day, presuming that the master was dead, the household group waited, as they had done through the years, amid the fragrance of incense, for the visit of his spirit to the family shrine. And while they kept vigil there, squatting on the matted floor, and watching the baby fingers of the candlelight caressing those little black tombstones on the "Buddha shelf," time itself stood still. Absorbed with the thought of their common loss, deep in a spell of pensive resignation, the members of the group were quite oblivious of all else. Even the sudden commotion in the street was lost on them—but all at once they heard the outer door sliding gently in its groove.

Then footsteps sounded in the entry, and a voice forever unforgettable called cautiously through the paper screen: "Excuse me. It is I!"

Legend has it that, long before his disappearance, the young noble of Satsuma had been tormented by religious doubts. Because the bonzes failed to resolve his perplexities, Anjiro consulted the Portuguese traders

Father Cosmos de Torres and Brother John Fernandez, his "other self"—besides the fugitive Anjiro, the latter's manservant, and another wandering Japanese who had been converted to the Faith, the saint boarded a Chinese corsair that had put in at the port of Goa and was bound for the islands of Japan. He set out on this new search for souls with as great a disregard for distance and peril as that of his immortal predecessor, Saint Paul. The "robbers' junk" lumbered across vast stretches of the deep, from April into August. Then at last Xavier reached his "longed-for land"—and the people into whose lives he came could never be the same again.

In Japan, Saint Francis Xavier began his brief apostolate of twenty-seven months at Kagoshima, probably in the home of Anjiro, now known as Paul of the Holy Faith. In keeping with his strategy of winning the common people through the nobility and intelligentsia —after all, the only strategy possible in feudal Japan— Xavier lost no time in soliciting the favor of the local daimio, or territorial noble. This ruler, apparently with a view to the benefits of trade with the visitors' countrymen, rather than from any conviction of the truth of Christianity, permitted the missioner and his companions to undertake the work of evangelization.

The new religion proved to be an amazing revelation to the Japanese. A personal God—yes, a Father in heaven—yearning with unutterable tenderness for His creatures here on earth; a childhood in the parenthood of this Supreme Being, intimately realized in human-kind, that "strong clod that plucketh down the neck of God"; the first feeble consciousness of love as great as that of Jesus hanging in anguish on the tree of Calvary, a love infinitely transcending the kindliness of Buddha seated in dispassionate ecstasy beneath the bodhi tree—these were all experiences of a new magnitude. And they were the revelations of a saint, the like of whom Japan has not seen since.

Xavier's own holiness of life accounts more than any-thing else for the success of his short ministry in Japan. Somehow the Japanese people must have sensed the sanctity of the man in whose apostolic heart raged such a quenchless fire that he has been called deservedly the "Firebrand of the Indies." True to the commission re-ceived from Saint Ignatius Loyola—"Go, set all ablaze!" —Xavier had rekindled the flame of faith throughout the Indies. Now, in the "Land of the Rising Sun," among a people who worshiped that great ancestral luminary, the fire in his Basque heart blazed up anew, as if in token of kinship with the sun. The Japanese could not have associated with Saint Francis Xavier without experiencing the thrill of the supernatural, just as men cannot consort with fire without feeling its heat.

Certain it is that Xavier knew little, if any, Japanese before he arrived in Kagoshima. True, there is a tradi-tion that, after forty days of language study, he was endowed with the gift of tongues, as he had been in

India. However, this appears to be merely a pious story, because actual records state that Brother Fernandez, in particular, often acted as interpreter for his saintly leader. If ever Xavier needed the gift of tongues, it was in Japan, for, as he declared, he could not help suspecting that the devil must have presided over the invention of the Japanese language, if only to hinder the preaching of Christianity! This anecdote is the more amusing, inasmuch as the saint's own Basque language is said to be so difficult that the Old Boy himself, after a fair trial of five days, declared it impossible to learn.

But the truth of God is not restrained by any wordy fetters. The Holy Spirit spoke through the inelegancies of Xavier's sermons, with unerring appeal to the hearts of his Japanese hearers. Men of good will believed the Gospel, and the number of converts mounted steadily.

This development was not lost upon the greatest single political power in the country; namely, the Buddhist priests. They soon realized that the new religion not only would take root in Japan, but eventually might even challenge their own supremacy. They had reasons for their fear, because many Japanese, contrasting the sacrificial lives of the foreign missioners with the luxurious existence of the bonzes, could not help being attracted to the religion that prompted such selfless devotion. Xavier's initial successes, then, were sufficient to stampede the bonzes into a campaign of opposition to Christianity.

Moreover, the Satsuma ruler had been disappointed by the Portuguese traders, who preferred to do business elsewhere, and he was easily prevailed upon to prohibit the exercise of the "foreign religion." In feudal Japan, the situation was *"cujus regio, ejus religio"*—"whose region, his religion." Therefore, fearful of official displeasure, not a few of Xavier's converts forsook the missioner. There was, however, a nucleus of at least two hundreds souls who remained faithful to the bitter end. They were Christians, not by the daimio's high permission, but by their own conviction. Magnificent people! The oldest convert among them was of only one year's standing; still, they were willing to jeopardize their very lives by adhering to a doctrine preached to them by a "southern barbarian," who had appeared in their midst like a bolt from the blue, no one knew whence.

His brief apostolate in the samurai stronghold of Satsuma thus abruptly ended, Xavier confided the infant church of Kagoshima to Paul of the Holy Faith. Then, with hopes still high despite this initial disappointment, the tireless missioner set out for the new Portuguese rendezvous in Hirado, near modern Nagasaki. There his compatriots welcomed him with the greatest honor, and this demonstration of respect made a deep impression on the local ruler. Immediately enlisting this official's good will, Saint Francis set to work again with the fine frenzy of zeal typical of the genuine apostle.

At Hirado, his apostolate was successful from the outset. But the genius of Xavier fretted for wider horizons. By winning the sympathy and understanding of the Japanese Emperor, he would accomplish, he believed, with one magnificent gesture, more than he ever could hope to achieve through the good offices of petty princes. Never a slave to indecision, he commended his little flock, and their rude chapel on the seashore, to Father de Torres; and accompanied only by Brother Fernandez, he took the road to the capital city, Kyoto.

En route to Miyako, as Kyoto was called at that time, Xavier visited the city of Yamaguchi, on the main island of Honshu. In that populous and luxurious provincial capital, styled in early missionary annals the "Corinth of Japan," the saint spent several months. But his labors there were fruitless. To intellects blinded by sensuality, the Gospel had no appeal.

In Yamaguchi, Xavier not only experienced very few consolations, but he suffered many tribulations. During his earlier labors, in the southern island, bonzes had openly hindered the success of his ministry, but there always had been limits beyond which they were unwilling to go. In Yamaguchi, however, the bonzes were bitterly fanatic in their opposition. They even incited the rabble against the foreign preachers, and more than once Xavier and his companion were spat upon and stoned in public. The meekness and good grace with which the missioners endured these insults were a much more eloquent testimonial to the truth of Christianity than any sermons they might have delivered to those deluded people.

Vain though his ministry was in Yamaguchi, Xavier was not dismayed. Ahead lay Kyoto!—the sacred city of the fabulous Mikado—Kyoto, about which he had heard so much from Anjiro on that memorable day in Malacca. In Yamaguchi he could fail, but in Kyoto—never!

It was then January of 1551. That winter, according to all accounts, was extremely severe. The dauntless apostle, however, made no special provision for his journey. Except for a parcel of roasted rice, viaticum he had none. This undertaking was to be the greatest adventure of his life, and the hardships associated with it were only condiments that gave it zest. His Mass kit on his back, Xavier set out for the capital. The road was infested with brigands and lawless samurai, but that fact did not matter. On to Kyoto!—"with no other guide and no other hope but God."

Some Japanese artist has painted a touching picture of Xavier toward the end of that journey. It depicts the saint running barefoot through the snow, in the wake of a nobleman's sedan chair, fearful lest he lose the way to the capital. It is one of those great works of art that make a man better merely for having beheld them. Years ago in Kyoto, the author first set eyes upon this painting, but it is still very vivid in his mind. Xavier is disreputably clad. His footprints on the white trail are tinged with red. He himself appears half frozen and completely famished. But oh, the face of him! It is gay, gay as never before; aye, gay as the countenance of no mere mortal. And such is the nature of his joy, that it suffuses his features with a glory, almost divinizing that emaciated countenance.

Emerging thus from the myriad dangers that peopled his path, through hostile villages where children jeered, and unfriendly wilderness where even nature seemed with deliberate intent to slow his apostolic quest, Xavier climbed the last rise. There in the distance, on the yon side of those encircling mountains, the vision of Miyako —enchanted city of black, serrated roofs, ubiquitously pierced by storied pagodas and lordly temples—broke upon his wishful gaze.

The weary apostle was to find in Kyoto not the goal of his dreams, but, perhaps, the bitterest disillusionment of his life. Capital of a country that was then a "weltering chaos of warring feudal atoms," the city bore the terrible marks of internecine strife. The Emperor was nominally sovereign, but actually he had been shorn of all authority by the daimios, who were practically supreme in their own states. Xavier did not have an audience with the "Son of Heaven." The bribe demanded by his venal ministers was too high; and besides, an audience would have been useless. The saint realized, in view of the conditions in Kyoto, that he must undertake the conversion of the individual rulers, if he hoped ever to win the Japanese nation to Christ.

Although the seed of the Gospel often falls by the inhospitable wayside—or, as in Our Saviour's parable, on rocky and impervious soil, or even in a tangle of briers, all of which mediums are hostile to its growth—it never fails to fall upon some good ground, whence it brings forth fruit a hundredfold. So it was with Xavier's preaching in unreceptive Kyoto.

One day, a blind minstrel mingled with the crowd who were listening to the lean, emaciated foreigner. The latter was the talk of the capital, and the blind man had come with the hope of hearing some amusing anecdote that might add to a minstrel's stock in trade. However, he remained to marvel at a revelation reaching down to him from heaven itself. He found himself asking, "Can such a thing be true?" And then, almost automatically, he was groping in the gray vastness toward the speaker, whose voice broke about him like the surging sea—for Father Xavier was addressing him directly, as if he were the only person there in that crowded public square.

Baptism followed later, and the blind minstrel of Kyoto, whose inward eyes had seen the glory of the dawn of faith, became Brother Lawrence, the first Japanese Jesuit. One day, Lawrence, too, would preach in Kyoto, and thousands of his countrymen would bless his name, because he shared with them that Light without which all men are blind. Except for that one gleam of meteoric splendor, the conversion of Lawrence, the Japanese troubadour of Christ, Xavier's hurried ministry in Kyoto was very disappointing.

Nothing daunted, the greatest missionary since the days of Saint Paul retraced his steps to Yamaguchi and began anew. The first time he had visited that gay and wicked city, he had been rejected as a poor pilgrim—or worse, as an unkempt madman. Where, then, only pomp and riches were esteemed, it were folly purposely to be poor. So Xavier appeared this time at the court of Yamaguchi in his capacity of Envoy of the Holy See and Ambassador Extraordinary from Goa. He, who without those ridiculous trappings of human office was glorified in heaven, needed them desperately to be acclaimed in Yamaguchi.

At last well received, the saint preached everywhere in the once-forbidden city during more than six months, and great was his success. The faithful multiplied amazingly, taxing the capacity of the old building that the daimio had placed at Xavier's disposal. Centuries later, after that church, known as the "Temple of the Great Way," should have crumbled to dust, the people of Yamaguchi would hallow its site with a monument to the memory of the great apostle who had preached *Tenshu*, the "Lord of Heaven."

3. The Rise of the Cross

ALTHOUGH XAVIER later avowed that never before had he experienced more profound consolations than those that came to him during his second ministry in the city where he had been so vilely misused on his first visit, the memory of his apostolate in Yamaguchi was marred by the reaction of the bonzes to his success. After Xavier had won the permission of the prince to evangelize his fief, the bonzes dared not openly abuse the missioner as they had done before. The days of rabble rousing were gone, but his enemies vilified the saint unmercifully.

Of course, they were only doing a very human thing, in a very human way. It was too much to expect that the bonzes would sit idly by and see themselves thoroughly though peaceably supplanted by foreigners, in their own citadels. Humanly speaking, the most lamb-like activity on the part of Xavier and his companions had to be met with the most unyielding opposition. To the bonzes, anything else would have meant the surrender of all that they held most dear. Agitation and outright opposition were bound to be their weapons.

True, there was a middle ground of compromise, on which Buddhist priests were definitely at home. When, about the year A.D. 550, Buddhism found its way into

Japan from China, by way of neighboring Korea, Shinto was the religion of the Japanese nation. The question of whether Buddha, the new deity, was superior or inferior to the sun goddess of Shinto eventually came to the fore. Logically, Shinto could not object to the Buddha's having a place in the sun, in a land where "the *kami* (gods) shone with a luster like that of fireflies"; but supremacy in its hierarchy of divinities, Shinto never could concede. Supremacy, however, was the essence of the controversy that ensued. Only a compromise would save the day, so the bonzes did not hesitate to identify Buddha with the sun goddess. The Sage of India, accordingly, was declared the reincarnation of a goddess of Japan!

Now, with the coming of Christianity, the Buddhist priests were not averse to another monumental compromise. Xavier's God, they declared, was identical with Buddha, and Christ was only one of his several reincarnations. Christianity, in short, was merely another brand of Buddhism! Xavier disagreed. The issue was clear-cut: two irreconcilable ideals were at stake. Opposition and open vilification ensued.

Unwittingly, the bonzes, by their campaign of vilification, did the hated "foreign religion" a distinct service. For apparently it was their systematic ridicule that altered Xavier's apostolic strategy, with such signal benefit to the whole vast Orient. The apostle was deaf to the mockery of his adversaries, until they began to de-

ride the Christian religion as a doctrine unknown to
the sages of China and therefore unworthy of credence
in Japan. Even then, no words of reviling rang in
the ears of that God-intoxicated man, as he stood in the
narrow lanes of Yamaguchi, a target for the abuse of
the priestly hecklers in the crowd. He heard only the
secret of the way to win the soul of Japan.

The civilization of the Japanese people, as Saint
Francis knew, had been borrowed largely from the
"Middle Kingdom"—China. Their spiritual culture, too,
had been imported, for the most part, from there. If
Christianity were to come to the Japanese from the same
fountainhead of wisdom, as the bonzes had suggested,
they certainly would embrace it. So Xavier was convinced. Accordingly, he entrusted his newest community to Brother Fernandez, and then set his face
toward China, on the road of no returning. Actually,
the "Firebrand of the Indies" had already set the land
of Japan ablaze, but he was not to realize that fact in his
earthly lifetime.

During Xavier's last visit to Goa, after his departure
from Japan and shortly prior to his tragic death on
Sancian Island, before the very gates of China, in 1552,
he provided for the recruitment of more missioners for
Nippon. Three fellow Jesuits arrived in Japan not long
afterwards, and joined the little band whose heroic
labors are as deserving of remembrance as are those
of Xavier himself. Without the self-sacrificing co-oper-

ation of his successors, the pioneering of the great apostle might have been in vain. Those brave, selfless missioners bore the heats and burdens of the day with amazing faith and fortitude, struggling for the extension of the kingdom of Christ, to the utmost limits of their human capabilities and endurance.

Years later, Nobunaga, one of Japan's great military leaders, while tracing on a map of the world the voyages of the missioners from Europe to his own country, would exclaim to Father Froez, "Perhaps this religion of yours *is* some fine thing!"

The newcomers went to work in Bungo, a "kingdom" in northeastern Kyushu. Bungo had been the scene of Xavier's last ministry, while he was waiting for the Portuguese ship that returned him to India toward the end of November, 1551. It subsequently became the first mission center of the Jesuit Fathers. In a departure from Xavier's strategy, the new missioners opened a hospital for the sick poor. This move, while highly successful among the lower classes, alienated the upper strata of society. As Xavier believed, all reforms in feudal Japan had to come from the top down. True, the ruling classes were not neglected, inasmuch as the missioners established in the city of Funay a college and university, which conferred the degrees of master of arts and doctor of divinity. But the caste system was strong in old Japan, and the upper classes did not take kindly to the democracy of the Christian religion. Fortunately, the ruler's son was converted in 1576, and practically the entire population of Bungo followed him into the Christian fold.

About the same time, Sumitada, ruler of Omura, a nearby fief in the southern island, embraced the Gospel. In consequence of this ruler's zeal, which surely was immoderate according to our standards, though hardly so according to the feudal norms of his day, thousands of his subjects joined the Church. It is only fair, however, to note for the record that many of those people to whom the Faith came without their seeking it, later learned to understand and appreciate the gift of God and they even gladly surrendered their very lives rather than relinquish it.

Sumitada's brother was head of the adjoining fief of Arima. Under "Prince Andrew," as he is known in missionary annals, the Faith likewise prospered. In Andrew's domain, the first middle school deserving of the name was established by the Jesuits, in 1579. It was there that persecuted Christianity was destined to make its last public stand in feudal Nippon.

As the earliest centers of Christianity were on the southern island—Kyushu—Nagasaki and its environs soon became the main stronghold of the Faith. Persecuted Catholics from other parts of the country naturally gravitated to the little fishing village where, through the good offices of Sumitada, a church had been erected. Because of this influx of population, Nagasaki quickly developed into a city of some thirty thousand souls, most of whom were Catholics. Despite the ferocity of subsequent persecutions, it never ceased to be the Rome of Catholicism in Japan.

While the missioners concentrated their efforts on Kyushu, the southern island, they did not forget the main island—Honshu—and especially the central provinces there. It was not until after the first decade, however, that the missioners organized a definite program for the conversion of the capital. Saint Francis Xavier's visit to Kyoto during the severe winter of 1551 had been wholly fruitless, as we have seen. It remained for one of his followers to succeed where he had failed.

In 1559, the Jesuit Father Vilella was received in audience by the Shogun (Ashikaga), who ostensibly ruled in the Emperor's stead. This shogun gave Vilella a house in the capital, permitting him to erect there a church, which was dedicated to Our Lady of the Angels. From this church as a mission center, Father Vilella and his companions evangelized Kyoto and its vicinity. In spite of fierce opposition on the part of the bonzes, whose very stronghold had been invaded by the preachers of the new religion, many of the nobility and intelligentsia embraced the Christian Faith. At least five churches were erected in the district comprising modern Kyoto and Osaka.

Some of Japan's greatest Catholics were the fruit of this second apostolate in Kyoto. Deserving of special mention are these two: Justo Takayama, one of Japan's outstanding confessors of the Faith; and Gratia Hosokawa, the ideal of samurai wifehood and motherhood.

Justo Takayama was the son of a great lord who had been converted to Christianity by blind Brother Lawrence, the Japanese minstrel who had been won to the Faith by no other than Saint Francis Xavier himself. Takayama was a zealous Catholic in every sense of the word. Not only did he promote the spread of the Christian doctrine in his own domains, but he was the guiding spirit in the conversion of several other prominent lords. A good soldier as well as a good Christian, he was proficient enough in the art of war to be appointed a general by Hideyoshi, Japan's greatest military genius. When, however, Takayama returned from the campaign in Korea, he met with the basest ingratitude: suspected of trafficking with foreigners, he was dispossessed of his ancestral estates and exiled to the Philippines. At the price of apostacy, Takayama could have returned to his native land; but for the sake of justice, this Japanese Catholic preferred to die in exile.

Gratia Hosokawa was a true daughter of the samurai. The only time she ever seriously transgressed the strict requirements of the "Great Teaching for Women" (the essence of which was sweet obedience) was when she was baptized without her husband's permission. On that account she was shamefully mistreated, until at length her husband recognized her virtues and then agreed to the baptism of their children. Later Hosokawa found himself on the losing side in the shogun's struggle for supremacy, and not wishing his faithful spouse to fall into the hands of his enemy, he requested a trusted servitor to behead her. In the midst of their blazing mansion, Gratia gathered her children about her and led them in a last prayer before the crucifix. Then this gentle Christian bowed her head to the thrust of the samurai blade.

The story of Lady Hosokawa has been dramatized. The climactic scene, in which for her husband's sake she is obedient even unto death, never fails to impress profoundly any Japanese audience.

As the tragic death of Gratia Hosokawa clearly reveals, the Island Empire at this stage of history was convulsed with feudal strife. The great daimios, completely ignoring the temporal authority of the practically imprisoned Emperor in Kyoto, were incessantly warring with their rivals. The powerful Buddhist monasteries, frequently at loggerheads with one another, were here and there involved in bloody conflict with the secular authorities. The preachers of a "foreign" religion, necessarily beholden to whosoever chose to be kind to them, hardly could appear upon such a hectic scene without running the danger of involvement sooner or later in the universal turmoil. Indeed, the specter of persecution of Christianity already loomed darkly in the background of this confused struggle.

Fortunately, at this critical juncture, when Japan was

threatened with complete disintegration, one of her greatest soldiers came to the fore, in the person of Oda Nobunaga. He was a pronounced enemy of the bonzes, who were continually meddling in affairs of state. During years of disorder many of the monks had armed themselves, so that some of the great monasteries housed thousands of trained fighters. These the superiors did not hesitate to employ whenever, in their dealings with the civil government, they needed a "persuader." Thus the famous monastery of Hiyeizan had dominated and terrorized Kyoto for a long time. With samurai forthrightness, Nobunaga plunged into the maelstrom of conflicting forces, and imposed a martial peace upon his bleeding fatherland.

It was with a view to harass the soldier-bonzes, rather than to second the new religion, that Nobunaga was favorable to Christianity during the fourteen years of his rule. The future was, indeed, full of promise for the propagation of the Faith. But this pleasing prospect suddenly faded when the doughty warrior died before his time. He was killed by one of his generals, who resented being used for a bass drum on an occasion when Nobunaga had quaffed too heartily at the amber fountain.

Under Nobunaga the Church had made giant strides in the central part of Honshu, Japan's main island. The dictator had fortified the hill country of Azuchi—overlooking beautiful Lake Biwa, in Shiga County, about an hour by rail from Kyoto. There in 1580, on the perimeter of this fortified zone, in sight of the towering walls of his own mountain castle, Nobunaga had presented the Jesuit missioners with a tract of land. On it they developed a thriving center of Christianity: their compound contained not only a church, but also a school—Japan's second middle school—and a novitiate for the training of native vocations to the priesthood and Brotherhood. Unfortunately, this splendid establishment was to vanish completely in the years of persecution.

Naught of it remains today, except a rice field that is known as "Daius"—a corruption of "*Deus*," the Latin word for "God." When in 1934 this territory was assigned by the Holy See to the American missioners of Maryknoll, the author went to Azuchi to identify the historic site of Daius. But God's field was not in bloom: there was not a single Catholic in the town.

The attitude of the new shogun, Hideyoshi, who inherited the mantle of Nobunaga after the latter's death in 1582, was much less favorable to Christianity. However, he was not ill disposed towards the missioners during the first five years of his reign. He gave them permission to preach throughout his domains, and it is said that he requested them to forward a copy of his decree to Europe as evidence of his good will toward the Christian religion. At first, the Portuguese Jesuits had labored alone in Japan; but during Hideyoshi's tenure of office, the Spanish Franciscans arrived on the scene.

The coming of the Spaniards was to complicate an already delicate situation.

Before proceeding further with our story, it might be interesting to glance at the record of missionary progress in Japan from the time of Saint Francis Xavier, up to this juncture. As early as 1582, thirty-three years after the saint's advent in Kagoshima, there were 150,-000 converts, according to the Annual Letter that the Jesuit Fathers sent to Rome. Of this total, 125,000 converts were in the southern islands, principally in Kyushu; and the remainder were in central Japan. There were forty Jesuits on the scene, several of whom were Japanese. Catholic churches totaled two hundred. By 1595, the number of believers had more than doubled. Among the converts were a number of distinguished people, including almost twenty feudal chiefs, not a few bonzes, and many scholars.

The Jesuit Visitor General, Father Valignani (bearer of the Annual Letter of 1582), was accompanied on his return to Europe by an embassy of four young Japanese nobles, sent to the Pope by the Christian daimios of Kyushu. A well-known Japanese painting depicts the triumphal progress of these young samurai through the streets of Rome, when two years later they were received in state by Gregory XIII. The spectacle of the youthful Orientals kneeling before the Papal throne, garbed in their gorgeous silken gowns, conspicuous by their strange coiffures and by the gold-encrusted

swords thrust into their girdles, brought tears to the
eyes of the aged Pontiff.

In the meantime, various factors, principally political,
were at work in Japan, tending to influence the shogun
against the new religion. These factors account for the
ruler's sudden about-face in 1587, when he issued an
edict prohibiting Christianity and commanding the expulsion of the missioners. This edict, however, was not
enforced immediately. Indeed, the persecution that it
foreshadowed was delayed about ten years, since Hideyoshi feared that oppression of the foreigners' religion
would divert from his realm the advantages of their
trade. But his prohibition of Christianity—simply another move in a political game at which the shogun was
adept—served to appease the bonzes, who had bedeviled
him incessantly. Moreover, consummate diplomat and
politician that he was, Hideyoshi knew that the threat
of enforcement of his decree would serve as a sword of
Damocles, guaranteeing the utmost circumspection on
the part of the missioners in the performance of their
ministry.

The shogun was correct in his surmise, for the
preachers of the Gospel thenceforth adopted a very
cautious attitude. However, although the tempo of
mission activity slackened considerably in the capital
and its vicinity, the bounding pulse of Catholic life in
Nagasaki, the "little Rome" of Japan, was slow to falter.
On Christmas Eve of 1594, over five thousand people

are said to have requested baptism, although Catholic services had been banned under Hideyoshi's decree. At the seminary on near-by Amakusa Island, more than fifty Japanese boys continued their studies for the priesthood.

As there were Christians in the court of the Roman emperors, so there were followers of Christ in the very household of the Japanese shoguns. It is known, for example, that there were at least two Christians in the inner circle of Hideyoshi's court. One of them was an admired master of *cha-no-yu,* the tea ceremony, which was the most fashionable diversion of Japanese society in the sixteenth century. Hideyoshi, like his predecessor, Nobunaga, was an enthusiastic votary of the tea cult, and maintained his own masters of ceremony to preside at the gorgeous tea parties that shoguns frequently gave.

Originally, there was nothing ceremonial about tea drinking in Japan. The Buddhist monks imported the custom from their contemporaries in China, who relied on the pale, green beverage to keep them awake during their long, nocturnal meditations. In a later stage of its development, tea drinking became a cultural pastime, which in the course of centuries was regulated by a strict code of ceremonies that emphasized profound respect for simplicity and antiquity. There is a tradition among the Japanese that, thanks to certain variations and interpretations introduced into the tea ceremony, probably by Hideyoshi's "tea master," the persecuted

Catholics of old Japan found in the ritual of tea drinking a memorial of the Mass, of which they had been deprived.

Despite his seeming toleration, Hideyoshi really was wavering between a policy of promoting foreign trade, on the one hand, and suppressing the "foreign religion," on the other. In October, 1596, an unfortunate incident occurred, which decided the issue in the shogun's mind.

A Spanish galleon, *San Felipe*, had run aground on the coast of Japan, and the pilot tried to intimidate the local authorities, who were bent on confiscating the ship. He threatened them with the direst consequences, if his vessel were not released. Spain was a mighty power, he bragged, and it had subjugated many nations. He went on to declare that the Japanese little dreamed how much they already had succumbed to the influence of his countrymen, for the missioners had long been preparing the triumph of their fatherland.

The lying Spaniard's boast was the straw that broke the camel's back. It convinced Hideyoshi that Christianity *was* the spearhead of an invasion, as its enemies had always declared. The tyrant believed that he had the admission from the mouth of a Christian, and his fury knew no bounds. He immediately ordered the arrest of the Spanish missioners, the Franciscans in Kyoto and Osaka. But greedy is the maw of a dictator's belated vengeance! Soon other innocents fell victims to the tyrant's wrath.

4. So Red the Rood

TWENTY-FOUR PERSONS—including six Spanish Franciscans, three Japanese Jesuits, and fifteen Catholic laymen, two of whom were mere boys—were condemned to mutilation and crucifixion when the active persecution by Hideyoshi began. In the prison of Kyoto, the lobes of the left ears of the victims were sliced off. Then the condemned men were exposed to the public gaze. Three together, they were forced into rude, cart-like vehicles, in which they were drawn through the streets of the metropolis, while a crier preceded them to attract attention. Subsequently, the martyrs-to-be set out, under heavy guard, on the long journey to Nagasaki, in the southern island—Nagasaki, soon to become the "holy land" of Christianity in Japan.

Not far from modern Kobe, the marchers were allowed a brief rest, and there a young man begged to join their company. The new recruit had been baptized only eight months before. A little farther on, another layman fell in with them. At length, all were carried by boat to the southern island. From Hakata (now Fukuoka) the twenty-six martyrs set out on foot for Nagasaki, arriving there three days later—February 5, 1597.

Twenty-six rough-hewn crosses had been erected on

the slope of Mount Tate (pronounced *Tahtay*), looking across the city to the sea. To the right and left of each cross stood a soldier armed with a lance. The twenty-six Christians were required to mount the crosses. With ropes, their wrists and ankles were bound to the cross-beams. Outstretched, the martyrs waited through hours of agony, for the glory to come. Toward evening the fateful word of command rang out, and the alert sentinels plunged their spears into the hearts of the first martyrs of Japan.

In all their ten centuries in the Island Empire, the Buddhist priests could point to nothing like the impassioned eloquence of crucified Paul Miki. That Japanese Jesuit Brother had preached in very truth "like dying man to dying men." Nor could the Buddhists boast of heroism like that of little Ludovico, who looked down from his cross in childish glee, completely oblivious of his heartbroken mother sobbing outside the bamboo barrier.

Two years after this massacre, Hideyoshi, the Napoleon of Japan, was gathered to his ancestors, and the Church had another respite—the calm before an impending storm. The new shogun, Iyeyasu, was not only an able soldier, but also a skillfull diplomat. Like his predecessors, he was desirous of maintaining commercial relations with the foreigners, and he tolerated the presence of the missioners as long as he could use them to ingratiate himself with the traders. Nevertheless, during the first ten years of Iyeyasu's rule the Church flourished. Although persecutions were waged by individual daimios in their own fastnesses, such was the progress of the Faith that the first decade of the seventeenth century deservedly has been called the high-water mark of Catholic missions in Japan. According to one record, the Japanese faithful numbered 600,000 souls during this period of history, although less than 500,000 may be a more exact figure.

Simultaneously, however, malign influences were furiously at work. First of all, suspicion of the foreigner, a suspicion characteristic of pre-war Japan—characteristic, indeed, of the whole Orient, inclusive of Siberia —had not abated in the least. True, the suspicions of the Japanese were not without some foundation in fact. Then as now, the medley of genuine piety, devotion, and self-sacrifice on the part of the missioners, and the shameless, un-Christian tactics of the nations from which they came, presented, at best, an enigma to intelligent Orientals.

Against these suspicions, the missioners were utterly defenceless. To be sure, they made mistakes of their own, mistakes that stemmed from overzealousness, and these did not help their cause. But it is stupid and vicious to contend, as some writers have done, that the persecuted missioners were more to blame for their sorry plight than were the monsters who harried them. Moreover, the fact of a common nationality was sufficient ground for condemning the pioneer missioners together with the unscrupulous foreign traders. The latter, like buccaneers everywhere, kept the port cities of Japan in turmoil, and some went so far, on occasion, as to carry off natives into alien slavery. At that time, as during the author's years in Nippon, the Japanese people hardly could be blamed for suggesting that the missioners would do better to go home and preach the Gospel to their own benighted countrymen.

The arrival of mission helpers of other nationalities, men who were less circumspect than the pioneer apostles, served to heighten the prevailing tension. Finally, the activities of most of these foreigners were staged in sections of the country that were far from the capital, and that enjoyed a greater measure of autonomy. Consequently, the allegiance of local rulers in the southern island, the stronghold of Christianity, was a burning question in the mind of the usurping shogun. The possibility that daimios of the south might unite against him had become a nightmare to Iyeyasu.

To make matters worse, at this uncertain juncture English and Dutch traders arrived on the scene, and took up with gusto a campaign of vilification against the Portuguese and Spaniards, in order to supplant the traders of those nationalities. In particular, Will Adams, a shipwrecked English mariner forced into the employ of Iyeyasu, was no friend to the Latin competitors of his own countrymen. Although Adams does not seem to have cherished any particular animus towards Catholicism and the Catholic missioners, he did much to unsettle the shogun's mind against all Portuguese and Spanish nationals.

Be it said to the credit of the Portuguese and Spanish adventurers, they never were prejudiced against the spread of the Faith. If missioners wished to follow them to new lands, in order to preach the Gospel of Christ, that was agreeable to the traders. Their galleons were not closed to God, if God did not disdain to walk their irreligious decks. Doubtless, the rulers of the missioners' homelands were not always single-minded. Doubtless, too, the compatriots of the missioners often saw, in the prospect of association with them, advantages of mutual support. Nevertheless, there was no intent on the part of any of the Portuguese or Spanish, positively to exclude the diffusion of the Gospel.

The late comers—the English and Dutch traders— offered the shogun the benefits of foreign trade without the drawbacks of a "foreign" religion. They were solely and brutally on business bent, even to the exclusion of religion. Indeed, the Dutch traders owed much of the singular toleration that they came to enjoy, to the part they played in the annihilation of the Christians of Shimabara. At any rate, the new arrivals were able to convince the shogun that toleration of the foreign religion was a price he did not need to pay for the benefits of foreign trade.

Principally, therefore, for political reasons, Iyeyasu was persuaded to proscribe Christianity. He issued an edict in 1614, ordering that all Christian churches were to be destroyed, and that all Christians were to recant or be exiled. Actually, many sterling Christians were deported to the inhospitable northern islands, while others found their way as far south as Macao and the Philippines. (In Macao one may still see the ruins of a church that was erected by some of those exiled Japanese Catholics.) All missioners were commanded to bid farewell to the land of their adoption. Over thirty succeeded in escaping deportation; and of those who were expelled, not a few managed to return. It is recorded that, during the ensuing thirty years, at least a dozen groups of missioners were smuggled in. Those who thus succeeded in penetrating Japan—probably one hundred—were eventually put to death for the sake of Christ.

Still, the full fury of the storm waited on Iyeyasu's death. That shogun had realized that the feudal chiefs, among whom not a few were Christians, sympathized with the common people, whose only crime had been to embrace a "foreign" religion that they believed to be true. It remained for the shoguns Hidetada (1605-23) and Iemitsu (1623-51) to initiate a persecution of Christianity as systematic and dreadful as any in the history of the world. On this point both foreign and Japanese writers agree.

A new department of government, called the "Christian Inquiry," was inaugurated under Hidetada. It was the business of this service to hunt down like wild beasts both foreign missioners and their converts, compelling them to renounce Christianity, on pain of torture and death. The "Inquiry" offered monetary rewards for the betrayal of the faithful; and these sums were successively increased, through the years up to 1711. In the extirpation of the "foreign" religion, modes of torture and execution proceeded from horror to horror. With an excess of sadistic cruelty, the persecutors actually vied with one another in perpetrating prolonged and frightful barbarities; they would not permit the dispatching of their victims at one blow. The persecution was one of the most savage of all history.

In a paper submitted years ago to the Asiatic Society Transactions, J. H. Gubbins has this to say in regard to the methods of the Japanese persecutors of Christianity: "We read of Christians being executed in a barbarous manner in sight of each other, of their being hurled from the tops of precipices, of their being buried alive, of their being torn asunder by oxen, of their being tied up in rice bags which were heaped up together, and of the pile thus formed being set on fire. . . . Some poor wretches by a refinement of horrid cruelty were shut up in cages, and there left to starve with food before their eyes. Let it not be supposed that we have drawn on the Jesuit accounts solely, for this information. An examination of the Japanese records will show that the case is not overstated."

In the systematic development of this scientific sadism, two refinements were outstanding. First, there was the fiendish technique of lacerating the bodies of the victims with bamboo saws, and thereafter plunging them, red and raw with wounds, into the boiling *solfataras* on Unzen. That "terrible mountain" seemed to steam to the very skies with its bubbling sulphur wells, which the Japanese even today describe as "hells."

The ultimate refinement was known as the "torment of the fosse." In this the hapless victim, completely swathed except for one hand left free to make the sign of recantation, was suspended head downwards in a pit five or six feet deep. The pits were often partly filled with offal. There in those black holes, many of our brothers and sisters in the Faith hung for as long as a week, exuding blood from mouth and nostrils, maddened by fearful pressure on the brain, until death mercifully released them from almost insupportable anguish. Often the persecutors prolonged the victims' agony by letting blood from veins that bulged black at their temples. It takes a steady nerve and a strong stomach even to contemplate such sickening tortures; but it ill behooves us to shrink from facts, in an age when Christians are again being persecuted in many parts of the world.

Some Japanese who had recanted under the "torture

of the fosse," later declared that "neither the pain caused by burning with fire, nor that caused by any other torture, deserves to be compared with the agony produced in this way." Yet Japanese history records the heroic martyrdom of a young girl who endured the anguish for fifteen days!

Lest any Christian escape the dragnet, the whole country was divided into units of five families, each of which was held responsible for the conduct of the others, under pain of punishment affecting the whole group. In practice, this meant that each family became the watchdog of the orthodoxy of four other families, in order to insure its own immunity from the rigors of the law. But the persecutors did not entrust the matter completely to the zeal of these "neighborhood groups," as they were called. Whenever suspicion attached to the beliefs of people in any community, the government conducted its own inquisition. During this process, which was known as "Image trampling," the entire population of the suspected quarter was compelled publicly to tread upon a plaque depicting the Crucified Christ or the Mother of God. Even babes in arms were obliged to place their tiny feet upon the sacred emblems.

Once the nation had been combed of Christians, the preservation of Buddhism, which had been recognized in the meantime as the state religion, was left to the bonzes. The latter required the Japanese people to appear annually at their local temples, in order to take a prescribed oath. This oath forswore all connection with the "wicked religion"—a term that the bonzes began to use for the Christian Faith. The registers of the temples are extant in many places in Japan; they are monuments to the persecuting zeal of the Tokugawa dynasty, a great family of politicians.

In Japan, as elsewhere, it was true that "the blood of martyrs is the seed of Christians." The persecutions carried out by the successive shoguns, after the death of Iyeyasu, intensified rather than diminished the zeal of the Japanese faithful. Indeed, so great was the enthusiasm for martyrdom among them, that Cocks, a Dutch witness, writing in 1619, could not help remarking that the persecutors actually tired of putting Christians to death.

"Such was their constancy," Cocks reported, "that their adversaries were sooner weary of inflicting punishments, than they were of enduring the effects of their [the persecutors'] rage."

How many Catholics were put to death during those bleak centuries, it is difficult to say. According to one Japanese record, 200,000 persons were punished for the "crime" of being Christian. Whether or not this punishment entailed death, is not certainly known; but there is good reason to believe that as many Christians sacrificed their lives in the course of these Japanese persecutions, as were martyred during the ten persecutions of ancient Rome. If, then, faith like this—and for their faith, contempt of life like this—is the stuff of the soul of Japan, who would not wish to have that nation saved for Christ?

We may not follow the long series of events that led to the extirpation of the Christian religion in Japan. But the final act of that great tragedy—the Shimabara Rebellion—is deserving of special mention. This revolt broke out on Kyushu, during the autumn of 1637. It did not originate with the persecuted Christians, but they were involved in it inevitably.

The uprising is traceable directly to the discontent of the general population of the fiefs of Arima and Amakusa Island, which long had suffered under the needless and senseless cruelty of their respective daimios. After the transfer of the daimio of Arima, the new governor dispossessed all the retainers of his predecessors. He reduced those samurai worthies to the humbler status of tillers of the soil, an occupation for which they had no training and little liking. The degraded and dispossessed soldiers, of course, made unsuccessful farmers. As such, they soon were unable to meet the impossible exactions of their new overlord, who demanded more and more taxes.

This monster, in order to spur the clumsy efforts of the samurai-farmers, subjected them to the ordeal of the "*mino* dance" in which the unfortunate victim was dressed in a peasant raincoat of straw, and set afire. What was only a diversion to the tyrannical overlord, often resulted in the fatal burning of the poor wretch condemned to undergo the torture.

When human nature could endure no more, the samurai-farmers of Arima rose in revolt. They were joined by the downtrodden, non-Christian peasants of near-by Amakusa Island; and also, by the persecuted Christians of both fiefs, who for years had been groaning under a tyranny too terrible for words. The insurgents probably numbered about forty thousand men, women, and children. They all took refuge in Hara Castle, an almost-impregnable, moated stronghold situated by the sea, in the district of Shimabara. There, on that rallying ground of the oppressed, where the first defenders of the people's rights in Japan rose against a villainous slavery, Christianity made its last public stand in feudal Nippon.

The besieged Christians fought under banners inscribed with the names of "Iezusu," "Maria," and "Santo Iago" (the latter the patron saint of Spain). In vain did the enemy, 160,000 strong, attack the castle. Time and time again they stormed the outer ramparts, only to be thrown back by the desperate men behind the walls. During three months the embattled peasants held the flower of the shogun's armies at bay. The courage of the besieged struck terror into the hearts of the Tokugawa generals, who became so frantic that they unashamedly enlisted the services of the Dutch in Hirado. Those good people from Europe bombed Hara

Castle from February 24 to March 12, but without making any appreciable breach in the fortifications.

In the course of the siege, a message was dispatched from the fortress, on the wings of an arrow. It explained to the attackers the motives of the entrenched Christians, and this testimonial will ever remain as a refutation of those who would question the sincerity of the early Japanese converts to Catholicism.

"We have done this," said the missive, "not with the hope of obtaining lands and houses, but simply because the Christian religion has been forbidden by the shogun. If we should continue to live as Christians, and these laws be not repealed, our bodies being weak and sensitive, we might sin against the Lord of Heaven. These things fill us with grief beyond endurance; hence our present condition."

At the height of the siege, the enemy commander promised amnesty to all non-Christians, as well as to all Christians who would abjure their Faith. When the outlook became desperate, the entire non-Christian element went over to their oppressors. For the Christians, however, there was no escape: after their epic struggle, they could hardly expect the leniency that they had been denied while they suffered unresistingly under the yoke of their persecutors. When at last the castle was taken by assault, on April 12, 1638, more than thirty thousand starved farmers, who had lived on grass during the last weeks of the siege, were put to the sword. The number included men, women, and children. Hara Castle was leveled to the ground, and a forest of human heads were impaled outside the city of Nagasaki.

Onlookers agreed that Christianity existed no longer in Japan. But the inhabitants of Shimabara could never be sure of that. For on summer nights, curious pinpoints of light, like many tiny stars twinkling through a distant cloudbank, ride the wavelets lapping at the ruins of Hara Castle. In vain have scientists explained that this seeming phenomenon is due to the phosphorescent emissions of a certain fish. To the people of Shimabara (among whom the author once sojourned), those twinkling lights on the restless sea will always be the souls of the besieged Christians, who chose to perish in Hara Castle lest they "sin against the Lord of Heaven."

5. *The Hermit Kingdom*

THE EXCLUSION of foreigners followed the extirpation of the "foreign" religion. At the outbreak of the great persecution, all Spaniards had been forced to leave Japan. Soon after the Shimabara Rebellion, with which they had nothing to do, all Portuguese were deported. In 1640, the Portuguese sent an embassy to the shogun to negotiate the renewal of commercial relations; but the ambassadors were arrested immediately, and soon afterwards were beheaded. To make the break with foreigners complete, the Japanese were forbidden under pain of death to go abroad. Indeed, it was a violation of law even to construct a boat large enough to carry one to an alien shore.

When foreigners were expelled, exception was made for a handful of Dutch traders. They were the men who, by their bombardment of the besieged Christians in Hara Castle, had won the right to special consideration on the part of the Japanese Government. They alone were allowed to remain in the country; but they were practically imprisoned, under most humiliating conditions, on a tiny islet in Nagasaki Bay.

Thus, the caprice of a usurping tyrant made seafaring Japan a "hermit kingdom." If Iyeyasu had succeeded in transferring the center of foreign trade from Catholic Kyushu to Tokyo, the capital of his own domain, he probably never would have adopted his closed-door policy. That policy ended Japan's best hope of empire, estranging her people from the West by a psychological void so vast that only ships of war could bridge it. Another probability is that Iyeyasu would not have undertaken the suppression of Christianity, which all along appeared to be part of the bargain. Thus, he would have allowed the Church time to become acclimated and to prove that it never was an Occidental invader of an Oriental culture. Throughout the next two centuries, however, the old Japanese proverb became literally true of Nippon: "The frog in the well knows naught of the great ocean."

During that long span of embalming years, when the land of the samurai had been quite forgotten by the Western nations, the Catholic Church in Japan lived on in the hearts of those who ardently desired the conversion of the island people to Christ. At intervals during the eighteenth century, Catholic missioners landed on the coast of Japan—only to be captured and put to death.

The most famous of those daring spirits was the Italian Jesuit, Father John Baptist Sidotti. The Japanese conjure up an hilarious picture of this young foreigner's arrival in their secluded country, in 1708. Set adrift in a small boat off the coast of Japan, Father Sidotti managed to reach land. Disguised in peasant attire, he followed an unsuspecting son of the soil down a country lane. Drawing near to the farmer, Father Sidotti cautiously hailed him in words that the priest had learned from old books in Italy.

The Japanese needed only one look at the smiling features beneath the wide-brimmed, straw hat. Rooted speechless to the spot for a moment, he could only gape at the apparition from the foreign world. Then, breaking into a mad run, as if pursued by all the terrors in his ancestors' dreams, the farmer galloped into a near-by hamlet with the breath-taking news that another "outside-country man" had penetrated the sealed frontiers of the "hermit kingdom."

The Japanese admired the bravery of Father Sidotti so much that they only subjected him to honorable detention, in spite of the harsh dictates of the law. But the young priest had not left his far Sicilian home for nothing. Before long he converted his jailer. Next, he won over the jailer's family. Then he persuaded people in the neighborhood of the prison to espouse the Christian religion. This activity was too much for the authorities, of course. Father Sidotti was thrown into a vile dungeon, where he was suspended head down until death wrote finis to the dramatic career of this unsung martyr of Japan.

But there were inheritors of Sidotti's matchless spirit, among the sons of the Mother Church of Christendom.

During those long, dark centuries, the Holy See never had forgotten the need of missions in Japan.

In 1844, young Father Forcade, a priest of the Paris Foreign Missions Society, landed at Okinawa, in the Ryukyu Islands. The French Government had signed a treaty of commerce with China, and, to support its officials in that country, had dispatched a naval squadron under the command of Admiral Cecille. The admiral, a good Catholic, was glad to send Father Forcade to Okinawa, aboard a corvette in charge of Captain Duplan. At Naha the latter disembarked the twenty-eight-year-old priest and his companion, Augustine Ko, a Chinese seminarian. The captain informed the island's governor that Admiral Cecille would appreciate any courtesies shown to Father Forcade, who enjoyed the dubious title of "Chief Imperial Interpreter."

The Japanese governor was terrified at this unexpected responsibility, but the French were in no mood to parley. Moreover, the island official was under orders from the shogunal government to tolerate the presence of the foreigners, if he could not prevent them from landing. Father Forcade tells us in his Journal that, when the ship's officers went ashore, they were met by a crowd of curious people who showed not the least sign of hostility, although the police beat them off with clubs. The shopkeepers are said to have refused money for the few purchases that the Frenchmen made. When the latter returned to their ship, they were surprised to find it filled with fruit and other gifts—proof that the isolation policy of the Tokugawa government was not popular with the Japanese people.

On the first of May, Father Forcade went ashore. He was treated kindly everywhere, despite the fact that his police escort held him by the arm, in an effort to restrict his travels. The policeman, hoping to impress the missioner with his tall tale of the people's hostility toward foreigners, demanded of a little knot of curious onlookers, "Aren't you afraid of this foreigner?" "Yes," one of them waggishly replied. "We *are* afraid of him— whenever he is with you."

At the end of the visit, as Father Forcade was waiting for the ship's launch, a cross chiseled into the pavement of the pier attracted his attention. "What sign is this?" he asked. The Japanese official whom he addressed was evidently embarrassed for a reply. That cross was a test and a trap: it had been graven there by an officialdom bent on obliging every Christian who landed at Naha to commit apostacy.

On May 6, 1844, the two Catholic heroes went ashore for a stay of two years. During that time they were to be interned in a secluded bonzery, in honorable confinement. The next morning Father Forcade was up at dawn, vesting for the Holy Sacrifice. He already had consecrated the mission of Japan to the Immaculate Heart of Mary. Now he began to read the first Mass celebrated in two hundred years on the very doorstep of that "hermit kingdom." But as he uttered the opening prayer, a Japanese guard rushed angrily into the dim room.

Augustine, the Chinese server, turned on the intruder reprovingly. "The master is praying to his God. Woe to you, if you dare to move! Down on your knees, or out of this room!" The guard sank to his knees. Japan heard Mass again.

On July 2, 1846, Father Leterdu arrived at Naha. He came to replace Father Forcade, who was about to leave for Hong Kong, where he was to be consecrated Vicar Apostolic of Japan. On September 5 of the same year, another young priest, Father Adnet, joined the lone missioner; but he lived for only two years. Dying of consumption, he had offered his life for the conversion of the people of Japan. Mayhap some American soldier of the Occupation force will chance upon an untended tomb near the bonzery, in a grove by the seashore. Tread softly, soldier, by that grave where sleeps this young recruit of a foreign legion more ancient than your own.

But we are getting ahead of our story.

The tourist in Japan who wanders off the beaten track to Shimabara, in the southern island of Kyushu, may see the pine tree from which hung the gong that rallied the shogunal armies to the tragedy of Hara Castle. That eternal evergreen is the symbol of a faith that never died. The knell of Christianity had struck, indeed, but the after-vibrance of that bell pulsed like a *Sursum Corda* throughout the Island Empire, for two centuries and more. The Japanese Church, as far as external organization was concerned, had ceased to exist. Priesthood there was none. Mass was only a word of foreign derivation. Except for Baptism, of which they had only a corrupt Latin form, the sacraments were the merest memories to the Japanese faithful. Only their faith remained.

But what a sterling faith it was! Without benefit of clergy, it was of itself dynamic enough to possess the souls of thousands of men and women, throughout two hundred years of isolation and systematic persecution, inspiring in them the deathless will to dare all dangers and suffer every hurt. Time and time again throughout that long Good Friday, martyrs set the blood seal on their faith; yet though the faithful perished, lavish in their sacrifice, their faith lived on—in the catacombs of humble hearts, unreachable, untouchable, and as indestructible as the faint perfume of musk in an ancient tomb.

Thus, the slow procession of the years filed past, until at length the long Tokugawa reign of martial peace and order came to an abrupt and disorderly close. Abroad in the land was a spirit of curiosity about the outside world, which did not at all comport with the prevailing seclusion. Ever since the opening of Nippon to the West, there had been Japanese devotees of European culture who, in spite of incredible difficulties, had kept alive the spark of learning. More than one of those zealous students paid for his curiosity with his life, during the centuries of isolation when the "Dutch factory" at Nagasaki was their only beacon of enlightenment. Intrepid seekers after truth, such Japanese were the leaven in the paste of Old Japan. Restive spirits, they fretted against the bars of their hermitage, until at last their country's soul was free.

By the relentless enforcement of exclusion edicts, the Tokugawa usurpers had succeeded in isolating Japan from the rest of the world. In achieving this end, they had done their country a sorry service. They had accomplished, indeed, a thorough reorganization of Japan's political and social structure; but otherwise, those two centuries of isolation proved harmful to the complete development of Japan. While other nations had gone forward by leaps and bounds in the fields of domestic enrichment, national prestige, and international relations, Japan had been seriously retarded. Other nations had been waxing virile and dynamic, while she immured herself behind sealed frontiers, setting the tempo of national existence without the slightest reference to the pace of the outside world. Mighty in her own conceits, Japan actually was woefully weakened by her long inertia, as subsequent events clearly showed.

It was concern over their country's retarded development that preyed upon the minds of those few Japanese who had contact with the Dutch merchants in Nagasaki. When, later on, intellectuals like Kaempfer, Tit-singh, and Siebold came from Holland and established residence on Deshima, these Japanese were confirmed in their fears. It might be right enough, they thought, for Nippon to isolate herself from the family of nations, and bid the rest of the world go by. But what would happen if the rest of the world refused to abide by this unilateral agreement? That was the haunting fear of those farsighted sons of Yamato who associated with the Dutch on "Forward Island," that ungenerous port-hole through which the Japanese gazed at the ocean of the world outside.

Toward the second half of the eighteenth century, the Occidental powers began to bestir themselves in the Orient. In promoting trade with China, they adopted a vigorous attitude that often smacked of aggression. Russian, English, French, Spanish, and American mer-chantmen began to appear in the waters of the northern Pacific, where they attempted to intrude upon the Jap-anese scene. These various, disconnected efforts to force the national gates of Japan were in vain. But that country was bound to be affected, sooner or later, by this impact of East and West.

In the middle of the nineteenth century, these hap-hazard attempts on the part of the Western powers to re-establish relations with the Island Empire took on a more definite complexion. Great Britain had brought China to her knees in the Opium War of 1839-42, compelling her to open five ports to foreign trade. The United States, France, and other countries, followed close on the heels of Britain, and concluded treaties affording themselves similar privileges. The next objective of the Western powers in their quest for opportunities of trade expansion was naturally Japan. Seeing the threatening turn that the international situation had taken, the Dutch on several occasions tried to acquaint the shogunal government with the true state of affairs. The Dutch advised a resumption of relations with the outside world, but the shogunate insisted on adhering to its exclusion policy. Thus, the reopening of the "hermit kingdom" waited on the initiative of the Americans.

The American Government's negotiations for the reopening of Japan were motivated principally by considerations of practical necessity, growing out of the rapid development of our trade with China. A direct shipping route had been opened between San Francisco and Shanghai, and on such a long haul there was a crying need of intermediate ports of supply and repair. Commodore Matthew Calbraith Perry was the man chosen by the United States Government to effect an understanding with Japan.

At the head of four men-of-war, Perry sailed into Yedo Bay on July 8, 1853, and anchored off Uraga. A few days later he delivered President Fillmore's letter to officials who, he had been led to believe, represented the legitimate government of Japan. Promising to return for a reply early the following year, he sailed away to the Ryukyu Islands. In February, 1854, the "black ships" of Perry loomed again on the Japanese horizon. The American squadron had been increased to seven ships. As far as the shogunal government was concerned, the die had been cast; the rulers realized that Japan was no match for the powers thundering at her portals. Representatives of the two nations assembled in Kanagawa, on March 8, and negotiated a "Treaty of Peace, Commerce and Navigation."

Thus Japan was reopened to the outside world in 1854. But it was only after the treaties of 1858 had been signed, that Catholic priests were allowed to re-enter the country, and then in the capacity of embassy chaplains. The discovery of thousands of descendants of the early Christians naturally prompted these chaplains to extend their spiritual ministrations to the Japanese people.

6. The Great Find

FATHER PETITJEAN'S five years in Nagasaki, as chaplain at the French consulate, had been a period of barren toil, as far as the Japanese people were concerned. He had met few who were even remotely interested in the religion that he represented. But in 1865, in the "Time of Sadness" (Lent), the priest experienced a great thrill of joy. On March 17 he noticed a little group of Japanese, men and women, gazing up at the cross that surmounted the modest church, which he had succeeded in erecting on a hill in Nagasaki. Father Petitjean hastened to invite the gazers to view the interior, and they eagerly accepted his invitation.

As the priest knelt with the Japanese, in the aisle, praying with all his heart for those people whom Xavier loved so dearly, one of the women approached and whispered to him, "The hearts of all here are the same as yours!"

The little group had come from Urakami, on the outskirts of Nagasaki, where long ago the twenty-six martyrs had been crucified by order of Hideyoshi. "At Urakami nearly all have the same heart as we," the woman added, to the priest's amazement.

But the Japanese Christians were wary. They asked to

see the Virgin's shrine. And they had more questions for the missioner.

The news of the little church atop the hill in Nagasaki spread rapidly among the neighboring villages. Soon another delegation of Japanese appeared at the church, and talked with Father Petitjean.

"Have you the same heart as that of Rome?" they asked the priest. "Is it the Teacher-King who sends you?" Their last query was indirect: "Have you no children?"

Father Petitjean's answers completely satisfied the inquirers. Lo, they had found the Faith of their fathers!

The missioners soon learned that Catholics of Japan had preserved their cherished legacy for more than two hundred years, without benefit of clergy. The great Saint Francis Xavier had foretold such glorious perseverance when, in writing to Saint Ignatius Loyola, in 1552, he said: "This Japanese people is the only one which seems to me likely to maintain unshaken the Christian Faith, if once it has embraced it."

Like the persecuted Christians of ancient Rome, the Japanese Catholics had led a "catacomb" existence. They had emerged from those dark ages, during which their persecutors actually tired of putting them to death, as luminaries in the firmament of mission history. True, they had not been obliged to take refuge in subterranean vaults, as had the faithful of Rome. But there are catacombs that are not under ground: the caverns of fear, doubt, gloom, and despair, which are tunneled in the hearts of persecuted men and women everywhere. So it was with the Catholics of Japan, hidden away in the hills and isles of Kyushu, where even in their solitudes they dared not utter the name of Christ, except with bated breath.

Only by honeycombing the walls of their little mud and bamboo huts with repositories for their sacred emblems had the Japanese Catholics been able to safeguard the externals of their Faith. Occasionally even today, these little sacred keeps of the persecuted Christians come to light when, in the southern islands, old homes are razed to make room for modern structures. The author remembers the minor sensation that ensued upon the discovery, less than ten years ago, of an ancient chalice in the wall of an old house in Kyushu.

After the great discovery in Nagasaki, about fifty thousand descendants of the early Christians were found throughout the south, especially on the Goto Islands— west and north of Nagasaki. When the news reached far-off Rome, Pius IX, the reigning Pontiff, wept to hear the story of these long-lost children of the Faith. Some of the newly found Christians, unfortunately, did not submit. Many of them feared that open avowal of their religion would bring down upon their heads the smoldering wrath of the ever-watchful authorities. And some of their leaders were loath to forego their preeminence. Notwithstanding, approximately forty thou-

of Catholics, to reap the harvest in reopened Japan. The first Protestants came from the United States as representatives of the Episcopalian, Presbyterian, and Dutch Reformed Churches. Christianity still was under official prohibition, and the non-Catholic pioneers had to restrict their apostolate largely to their own countrymen. In the meantime, they worked with a keen eye to their future ministry among the Japanese. Evangelists of other Churches, especially the Congregational, Methodist, and Baptist, followed in the wake of the first arrivals, and joined in the work of preparation.

The baptism of the earliest Protestant convert took place in 1864. The first native church was organized in 1872. The American Baptists undertook the translation of the Bible, and this classic of the Meiji Era appeared in 1887. In an age when westernisms were fairly worshiped in Japan, the English-language classes conducted by Protestant missionaries were crowded. Those Bible classes—for such they were, essentially—proved a tremendous help in the diffusion of Christian doctrine, and the part they played in the phenomenal Protestant activity that was soon to ensue can never be overestimated.

In keeping with the current emphasis on education, the Japanese Government welcomed professional men, particularly from America, Canada, England, France, and Germany. Many of these men were Protestants, who were thoroughly mission-minded. Those educators scattered throughout the cities of Japan, founding little groups of lay apostles among their pupils. An outstanding example of those mission-minded Protestants was Captain Jayne, an American professor of science, who so influenced his young proteges of the samurai class that, during five years, more than forty of them became Christians. Of that number, not a few undertook the study of theology to prepare themselves for the Protestant ministry, in spite of the most unyielding parental opposition—which frequently culminated in disinheritance of the young seminarians.

The educational endeavors of Protestant missionaries met with signal success. In 1875, the foundations of Doshisha University were laid in Kyoto, by Doctor Joseph Hardy Neeshima, the first native Protestant pastor. Doshisha University was the first of several Christian colleges, which later were destined to receive official recognition by the Japanese Government. From the halls of those colleges would eventually go forth, into a non-Christian milieu, thousands of young men and women sympathetic with, if not converted to, the Faith of Christ.

In the meantime, Catholics were consolidating their work throughout the Empire. Until 1876, only priests of the Paris Foreign Missions Society—that venerable French community whose martyred sons have hallowed the mission fields of the whole Far East—had labored in Japan. But soon afterwards, those first Catholic apostles of modern Nippon were joined by co-laborers of other communities, especially Spanish Dominicans, German Franciscans, and French Cistercians.

Although for a short period the Protestant missions had a monopoly of the Western type of education, efforts along educational lines were launched early by the Catholic Church. In 1888, the Brothers of Mary arrived from Belgium and initiated an ambitious program of primary and middle schools for boys. Some of Japan's most outstanding Catholics have been graduates of the Brothers' Morning Star School in Tokyo. Catholic Sisterhoods, too, were soon at work, organizing primary schools and academies for girls. The Mesdames of St. Maur, the first Sisterhood that undertook educational work in Japan, were active as early as 1872. The excellent institutions of learning conducted by this community—like those founded later by the Religious of the Sacred Heart and the American Sisters of Notre Dame—have graduated hundreds of girls whose influence has been considerable among the elite of Japan.

The Japanese Government, although it had embarked upon a thoroughgoing program of its own, highly appreciated the missioners' endeavors for the advancement of education. On this account, despite the fact that prejudice against Christianity was still strong, the official attitude was one of toleration, and even of encouragement. Yet the prejudice was there, deep-seated. The non-Catholic newcomers tried to explain it away as an inconsequential survival from persecution days, and consequently as something solely attributable to the "old doctrine." This, of course, afforded a clever escape for their own "new doctrine." But the fact is that the Japanese sentiment was rather anti-Christian than anti-Catholic. New Japan was as easily scandalized by the un-Christian example of nineteenth-century Protestants, as Old Japan had been by the disgraceful conduct of sixteenth-century buccaneers who claimed to be Catholics simply because they were born of Catholic stock. Oh, tragedy past telling! Christ, our Lord, is crucified—even to the end of time.

The Japanese Government's religious policy, following the downfall of the shogunate and Nippon's reappearance upon the stage of Western civilization, was identified with the restoration of Shinto, the original cult of Japan, to a place of primacy. Shinto was officially recognized as the state religion. This meant that Buddhism, as well as Christianity, was slated for the official discard. Unfortunately, this governmental emphasis on the primacy of Shinto was an outgrowth of the chauvinistic sentiment that was abroad in Japan at that time, and it did not augur well for the future.

This incipient governmental opposition to all religions except Shinto, served to galvanize the Buddhists into measures of self-preservation. As for Christianity, Japanese officialdom received considerable unsolicited enlightenment from foreign powers, to the effect that persecution of religion was regarded by all civilized nations as simply barbarous. Thus, the Japanese Government was induced gradually to modify its stiffening attitude toward Christianity; and the promulgation of the Constitution of the renowned Emperor Meiji, in 1889, signalized the complete emancipation of the three great religions of Japan.

The Shinto campaign for primacy, on the one hand, and the Buddhist and Christian struggle to survive, on the other, naturally gave rise to some interreligious agitation; but followers of the three religions soon were distracted from these lesser worries by a common peril. There was a growing indifference to things long held sacred, and it was accompanied by a widespread lack of practical religion. This situation stemmed from a popular heresy imported from abroad—the theory that religious instruction is incompatible with higher education. Much of this indifferent and irreligious attitude grew out of the materialistic "English philosophy," embodied in the works of Mill, Herbert Spencer, and others, who soon became popular among the idea-starved intelligentsia of Japan. But an even more unfavorable influence was exerted by certain English, Scotch, and German teachers, who, in their lectures, openly inveighed against Christianity.

This conduct led Akamatsu, a learned Buddhist bonze in Kyoto, to declare, "It is your own philosophy that Christianity will have to fight, here among the educated; not Shinto or Buddhism."

Thus, many young Japanese, infected with the virus of materialism and agnosticism, began to doubt the existence of God and the immortality of the soul, with a resultant loss of interest in the moral precepts of religion. Buddhism and Christianity, in particular, agreeing that without the hope of immortality there can be no genuine righteousness, came to realize that a live-and-let-live policy must be the absolute minimum of co-operation. This understanding, if such it may be called, was timely; because at the outset of the twentieth century the Japanese, despite the materialism of so many of the student class, were soul-hungry as never before. That was not because the Gospel of salvation had been tried and found wanting, but because it still was desperately untried.

The average truth-seeking Japanese, faced with the divisions that Protestantism had introduced under the name of Christianity, either was too bewildered to venture into the labyrinth, or emerged from it with the resolution to forget forever the odyssey of his soul. Catholicism had the plenitude of truth, but the "old doctrine" lacked a certain glamour that was associated with Protestantism by reason of the time and circumstances of the latter's appearance on the Japanese scene. This situation was enough to deter many Japanese from an inquiry into the claims of the Catholic Church.

By 1894, New Japan had gone far toward completion of her internal reorganization along Western lines. She then was able to give her attention to the problem of adjusting herself to the outside world.

First of all, Japan had to consider her relation with neighboring Korea, the country across the straits. That "Land of the Morning Calm" long had been a bone of contention between Japan and China. Those two countries had succeeded in adjusting their differences temporarily, by the treaty of 1885, but the situation remained precarious. That was partly because of the unstable conditions in Korea; partly because of the friction between Japan and China; but chiefly because of the general uneasiness over the aggressive policy of Russia. Then, as now, the latter's intrigues in Seoul, the capital of Korea, were notorious.

When, finally, the Korean factions resorted to armed strife, both China and Japan rushed troops to the scene. China, denying the fiction of Korean independence, which Japan had been anxious to maintain, increased her garrison, despite warnings from Tokyo. An armed clash between the forces of the two occupying powers occurred, and war was on. To the amazement of China, the "island dwarfs" were easily victorious. Then, by the treaty of Shimonoseki (1895), the independence of Korea was recognized by China. Japan was awarded the Liaotung Peninsula (in southern Manchuria), Formosa, and the Pescadores, besides a large indemnity.

A coalition of European powers, however, promptly forced a retrocession of the Liaotung Peninsula. A few years later, to Japan's great chagrin, Russia, through a process of devious duress, succeeded in obtaining from China the lease of Port Arthur and Dairen, in the very territory that China had withheld from victorious Japan. What Nippon did not already know about the tortuous ways of international diplomacy, she learned on that occasion. Consequently, the Occidental powers had no right to be surprised when Japan, following the pattern set for her, annexed Korea in 1910, despite all her previous protestations concerning the independence of that unhappy land.

Naturally, the Japanese people were disappointed over the outcome of the war with China. But when the Liaotung Peninsula, the best fruit of their hard-won military victory, was snatched from them on ostensibly virtuous grounds, only to be awarded to undeserving Russia, their indignation knew no bounds. For them, it was proof positive that might makes right in the sphere of international relations—all the high-sounding pronouncements of Occidental statesmen to the contrary notwithstanding. The reader easily can understand the impact that the un-Christian actions of so-called Christian governments made upon the receptivity of the Japanese people. Christianity, still identified in Japanese minds as a foreign importation, could make only the poorest progress in such an atmosphere of disillusionment and distrust.

It was the old story all over again: in the nineteenth

century, as in the sixteenth, the people of Japan were led to reject the Christian religion chiefly because it was preached by foreigners whose motives were suspect on account of the shameless tactics of the countries from which they hailed. However, during this period of reaction when the Christian Faith gained ground so slowly in Japan, there were in that land Westerners whose names shine like stars in the firmament of mission history. Those men labored with admirable zeal to re-mold not only the religious thought, but other phases of Japan's national life.

Among Catholics, for example, there was Father Villion, a missioner for whom the Japanese people had the greatest admiration, and to whom, in his own life-time, they erected a monument in Yamaguchi, beside the memorial to Saint Francis Xavier. Father Villion labored in Japan for more than sixty years, after a brief period spent in the missions in China. School boys and girls, eager to hear the forgotten idiom of their samurai forebears, used to flock around the aged French priest when, bent double with the weight of years, he preached in the green groves of Nara. Father Villion and priests like him have raised more churches in sweat and blood than we, their successors, ever can hope to rear in brick and stone.

Another memorable figure associated with the Catholic missions of this period was the well-known *Père* Fage. Like Father Villion, he was a member of the

Paris Foreign Missions Society. In contrast with Father Villion, however, *Père* Fage was only beginning his apostolate when his venerable co-worker was entering upon the twilight of a long missionary career. In his later life, *Père* Fage was a familiar sight on the docks of Kobe, where he used to meet the young missioners from America en route to their posts in the Orient.

Many a man in far corners of the globe remembers the splendid church that the old French priest erected at the cost of much worry and toil, but few realize how much that edifice was a part of his very life. During the second bombing of Kobe, the vicinity of *Père* Fage's church was ringed with fire. When the incendiaries began to fall, his neighbors fled to the hills. They streamed past the old missioner's church, calling to him to run for his life. But the jaunty little man in the worn soutane just stood there, serene and smiling as always. How could he forsake the hallowed shrine in which the candle of his life had burned for so many years? No, he would not go.

With the missioner were his aging catechist, Mr. Furuya, and the latter's wife. *Père* Fage bade Mrs. Furuya join the crowd that was hurrying past the gates to the near-by hills, but she refused unless her husband would go with her. Faithful Mr. Furuya, however, demurred, unless *Père* Fage, too, would go with them. But the old missioner would not leave his church. It was too much a part of him. Very well—then no one would go. Three together, they knelt before the Blessed Virgin's altar, where they often had knelt before.

Soon the sacrilegious fire came screaming down the aisles. From her far height of glory, the Lady in whose hair the stars of heaven shine, must have beheld with eyes of unutterable compassion the holocaust before her Kobe shrine. After the fire had died down, survivors went looking for *Père* Fage—looking through the heap of ruin that was his church. And they knew that they had found him, there before the charred outline of the Virgin's shrine, when they came upon that little mound of ashes, "oh, so white!"—to hear them tell it, "whiter than the ashes all around."

Among the Russian Orthodox, who had established their first mission in Japan as early as 1861, no name is more illustrious than that of Father Nicolai, who later was consecrated Bishop of Tokyo. His cathedral, erected in 1891, was a little gem of architecture, which Chamberlain described as "the only ecclesiastical edifice in Tokyo that has any pretensions to splendor."

Among Protestants, too, there were shining examples of missionary zeal. Mention already has been made of Captain Jayne and Doctor Joseph Neeshima, two selfless men whose passion was the propagation of the Gospel. Deserving of greater remembrance than we can give them here, are the names of the venerable Doctor Hepburn, to whom we owe the romanization of the Japanese language; and in more recent times, the

Reverend J. Batchelor, apostle of the aboriginal Ainu in the northern islands; Captain Bickel, the brave pilot of the *Fukuin Maru* (Ye Goode Ship Gospel); and that grand old lady, Alice Denton, the matriarch of Kyoto.

In spite of the heroic labors of the missioners, the propagation of the Christian Faith was attended with comparatively scant success during the nineties. What a change had taken place since the eighties! During the decade from 1878 to 1888, the progress of the Faith had been so phenomenal as to lead many observers to entertain the thought of Japan's conversion to Christ by the turn of the century. Under the new Constitution, Christianity not only was immune from all persecution, but, in the national enthusiasm for change, was welcomed by people in all walks of life. The official attitude was one of favor. Not a few leaders of Japanese thought even went so far as to advocate the adoption of the Christian religion, if for no other reason than that it might be a bargaining point in Japan's negotiations with the Occidental powers.

The year 1888, however, witnessed a distinct reaction. Because of her failure in negotiating a revision of the unequal treaties, Japan's pride had suffered a grievous hurt. Those who had advocated the adoption of Christianity for purely utilitarian reasons, then turned their backs upon it. The official attitude became one of self-sufficiency, and reliance on the national heritage, rather than wholesale acceptance of innovations from abroad.

7. *Again the Samurai Sword*

THERE WERE, of course, a number of factors that obliged Japan to adopt the attitude of self-sufficiency. For example, Japan saw entrenched in Manchuria an alien and aggressive power, which the other Occidental states did not seem anxious to restrain. Russia, impinging upon Manchuria and intriguing against a weakened Korea, appeared to be a distinct menace in Japanese eyes. War was inevitable, although Japan left no stone unturned in trying to forestall it. Russia contemptuously refused to negotiate, thus driving the Japanese people into the arms of the *Sat-Cho* group of extremists, who advocated a radical solution of all outstanding differences between the two countries.

Hostilities broke out early in 1904, and continued during more than a year. Then Russia was obliged to sue for peace, although Japan herself was not far from the brink of disaster. As a result of the successful conclusion (1905) of the Russo-Japanese War, little Nippon rose to the position of a world power, with consequent improvement in her international prestige. Her internal economy, however, was in a precarious condition.

The Japanese people were incensed and disgusted at the terms of the Portsmouth Treaty, which provided no indemnity whereby they might liquidate the costs of the war. So great was their indignation that, when they were prevented by the police from airing their grievances at a mass meeting in Hibiya Park, they burned down nearly every police booth in the city of Tokyo. Moreover, the newly acquired territories turned out to be liabilities rather than assets, and the maintenance of large armies to police them simply pyramided deficit upon deficit. Trade and industry, since they could be developed only on borrowed capital, offered no amelioration of the situation. All in all, the years of the decade after the treaty were uneasy ones for the Japanese people, during which their attention was riveted on the harsh exigencies of the times.

Burning under the smart of wrongs, real or fancied, which they felt had been visited on them by the nations of the West, the Japanese were in no mood to yield to Occidental notions of religion and morality. Then, with 1914, came World War I, and in its wake a definite lull in missionary activity. During the final stage of that great struggle, even European missioners laboring in the distant Orient were mustered out by their respective governments. Not a few mission stations were abandoned because of lack of personnel, while many others necessarily were left in charge of lay workers.

After the war, missionary effort was concentrated for some time on the recovery of lost gains, rather than on new developments. Whereas Catholic missions, for the most part, had been entrusted to European personnel, Protestant missions had been principally in the hands of Americans. Thus, the Protestants had been able to maintain the essential continuity of their work, while the Catholic program had received a distinct setback. Eventually, the missionary movement regained its momentum, but mission workers discovered then that the receptivity of the Japanese people had been affected by vicissitudes attendant upon the war.

During World War I, as we know, Japan had been able to recoup her resources. Shipping and industry had boomed enormously, thus affording her an unprecedented prosperity. Unfortunately, this upsurge was not to last. It was only a sunny peak between two valleys of titanic gloom.

The industrial boom that followed the first World War had affected Japan's economy adversely. There were people who made fortunes, of course, but they were comparatively few (not more than five hundred families); whereas, the vast majority did not so much as taste the sweets of wartime prosperity. Prices had outstripped wages, and as usually happens under such conditions, the people's morale was undermined. A rash of strikes ensued, and the whole nation was in a state of ferment. It was during this crisis that the "great earthquake" of 1923 occurred, snuffing out the lives of 100,000 people and toppling into ruins much of the industrial edifice of New Japan. Before the unfortunate nation could recover from the cataclysmic blow, it found itself in the midst of a world-wide economic depression.

Japan's courage was at a low ebb. The sea of hardship that had engulfed her people confused her political thinking, and she was willing to turn to any quarter for succor. Communism reared its ugly head, screaming at the wanton waste of the people's substance by callous and stupid bureaucrats. Finally, army leaders of the samurai clans of Satsuma and Choshu rebelled in open disgust against the mismanagement of the government, and took matters into their own hands. After removing from the national scene, by the time-honored avenue of assassination, several statesmen whom they regarded as too susceptible to foreign pressure, the military initiated various measures of agricultural reform. In this way, they won the good will of the downtrodden peasant class. Then they staged a successful coup in Manchuria, creating an outlet for the whole nation's pent-up energies. Thus it was that the samurai, who had seemingly disappeared in the ruins of feudal Nippon, came into his own once more. Though his ancient trappings had been modernized, he was still his country's inexorable sword-arm.

After the successful outcome of the so-called "Manchurian Incident," in 1931, the star of the Japanese military definitely was in the ascendant. Nothing succeeds like success, indeed. The militarists of Japan, fresh from their conquests on the Asiatic mainland, were able to launch a barrage of shameful impositions upon their fellow countrymen in order not only to consolidate their gains, but also to pave the way for future imperialistic ventures. At that stage, perhaps, they did not contemplate a violent overthrow of the government and the establishment of an absolute dictatorship. But certainly they could be relied upon to take full advantage of their strengthened prestige, if ever the occasion should arise.

Loss of Manchuria, the foothold of empire, had become identified in the minds of the Suetsugu-Hashimoto-Doihara gangsters with the inevitable loss of the "face" of Japan—not to mention the "face" of the Japanese Army. It was not surprising, therefore, that the military party insisted on making consolidation of the new state of Manchukuo their country's pivotal policy. Accordingly, they proceeded with almost psychopathic zeal to secure the Manchukuoan bastion by bleeding their own country white.

In the period between the World Wars, Japan, much as had other nations in the past, presented the appearance of a diminutive figure fairly dwarfed by the enormous bundle of empire on its back. Year after year, the military made increasing demands upon the national budget, ruthlessly encroaching upon the allotments of other departments of the government, until more than half of the entire national income was earmarked for military expenditures. This one-sided finance adversely affected the whole economy of the country, and soon engendered open criticism. To stem the rising tide of opposition, the military, after a preliminary period of dual government, seized complete control of the nation. Government by assassination became the order of the day.

Working through the *Kempeitai*—Japan's own Gestapo—the new masters of Nippon proceeded to stifle the pitiful stirrings of unrest on the part of the people. Notorious firebrand groups, such as the Black Dragon Society, the Blood Brotherhood, the National Soul Salvation Society, the God-sent Troops, besides an assortment of patriotic gangsters operating as individuals, were deputed to kill off outstanding liberals who refused to be bludgeoned into silence. This underground reign of terror finally exploded into open violence in February, 1936, when soldiers of the First Division raised the standard of revolt. Foreign Minister Saito, Finance Minister Takahashi, Grand Chamberlain Admiral Suzuki, Inspector General of Military Education Watanabe, were assassinated. Unsuccessful attempts were made on the lives of Saionji (the Elder Statesman), Count Makino (Lord Keeper of the Privy Seal), Premier Okada, and others, all of whom had incurred the suspicion of the "young officers' clique."

The nation was rudely shocked by the spectacle of mutinous troops entrenched in the very heart of Tokyo, in complete defiance of the Emperor's orders to disband. In an emergency session of the Diet, Kunimatsu Hamada denounced the army's high-handed tactics in a fiery address that brought his colleagues streaming down the aisle to shake his hand. "Go and commit hara-kiri!" he cried to the War Minister, Count Terauchi. Thereupon the Cabinet, fearing assassination, chose to commit political suicide instead, by resigning en bloc. Hamada's ringing denunciation of the military sounded the death-knell of civilian opposition.

The Chinese had replied to the seizure of Manchuria by a general boycott, which reduced Japan's exports to one sixth of their annual total. Japanese troops, seventy thousand strong, had landed at Shanghai and had driven the Chinese 19th Route Army from the vicinity of the International Settlement, bombing Chapei to rubble. Then an agreement had been reached, terminating both boycott and hostilities, but leaving another wound to rankle in the breast of China.

The Manchurian adventure had been a costly one, and the Japanese Army soon attempted to recoup some of its lavish expenditures by encroaching upon the provinces of North China. The Chinese, whose national consciousness had been awakening rapidly under the impact of Japanese aggression, stood firm against this threatened invasion of the cradle of their ancient civilization. The Japanese civilian government reacted mildly enough to this rebuff, but not so the military; the latter apparently had decided to act before the renaissance of China could materialize. On the night of July 7, 1937, the inevitable

"incident" occurred. Japanese troops on night maneu-
vers exchanged fire with a Chinese outpost stationed at
Lukouchiao Bridge, near Peiping. The Chinese, by this
time thoroughly disgusted with appeasement tactics, did
little to localize the fighting, and Japan, for reasons of
"face," found herself committed to a showdown. Thus
began the so-called China Emergency, which four years
later would fit into the crazy-quilt pattern of World
War II.

With the whole Far East on fire, Japan's khaki-clad
jingoes seemed bent on enjoying a superlative field day,
even if they had to burn down their own "house" in
order to make a success of it. A high-handed policy
toward the personal and property rights of foreigners in
China, aggravated by a succession of "incidents" capped
by the deliberate sinking of the American gunboat
Panay, brought Japan close to war with the United
States, Great Britain, and France. As the conflict with
China progressed, Nippon gradually was geared to a
wartime economy. In the process of this nation-wide
regimentation, there was no department of the people's
life that was not affected.

Religion, like everything else, was simply grist for the
mills of overweening nationalism. Shinto, the original
religion of Japan, was the very stuff out of which had
evolved the gods of the warmongers in boots and spurs.
To all intents and purposes, Shinto was the state religion.
Japanese Buddhism, unprincipled always, was agreeable

to further compromises. This left Christianity as the real target of the reforming zeal of the militarists, who sought to prostitute all religion as a mere tool of aggression.

We are, in part, the products of our age. In an era of appeasement, unfortunately, there were not a few Christians in Japan who were not courageous enough—or should we say, reckless enough?—to gainsay the jingoes who were intent on subordinating the Church to their own narrow, nationalistic program. Even in high places, there was a great deal of wishful thinking: the furtive hope that, somehow or other, the crisis might never mature, and that the Church might be able to get along on a friendly basis with those who were set on her destruction! In all this artless thinking, there was a pronounced tendency to identify the miserable surrenders of appeasement with the delicate distinctions of practical prudence.

There were, of course, many generous souls whose love for Christ never was marred by any willingness to compromise. Their convictions needed no rarefied reasonings to justify them: come rack, come rope, they were Christians, and they were resolved to remain such. But the empire builders had tested what the ruling clique thought was religion, and it had been found weak. Actually, the rulers had not clashed against the buckler of true religion: their jousting had been only against the armor of religionists. But having found the latter fearful and prone to compromise, the Japanese totalitarians undertook to regiment religion itself.

To be sure, they did not embark upon a violent blood-and-thunder persecution of the ancient type. Religious persecution, except in such backward states as Russia and Titotalitarian Yugoslavia, has been streamlined and superficially humanized. No more do persecutors drag people through the streets and publicly behead them for their faith; now the technique is more genteel. Today's persecutors only snatch people from the light of day, bind them with gyves of steel in sound-proof dungeons, and there systematically, even scientifically, starve or torture them to death. Even so, the emphasis is not on making a martyr out of a man, so much as making a confessor out of him. Keep him alive! Yes—and by a refinement of evil, oblige him to accept "voluntarily" whatsoever contrary dogmas the persecutors may choose to define.

So it was in Japan, during those troubled years preceding the outbreak of World War II. Ostensibly, the leaders did not seek to martyr anyone: they only desired to oblige people to do voluntarily what those people preferred not to do even under pain of death.

First, then, in the order of belief, the ruling clique proposed a modernized version of the myth of the Emperor's divinity—an absurdity that the Emperor himself never seriously entertained. The Ministry of Education, in a brochure intended for the eyes of university professors, formally declared that the Emperor of Japan was a "living deity." In the same publication, however, it was stated that the Emperor was not thereby declared to be divine in the sense of the Supreme Being of the Christians. This reservation, authored by civilian members of the government, was not to the liking of the jingoes, whose secret aim was to establish the Emperor as a kind of Supreme Being in relation to the Japanese.

Too clever not to see the rational difficulties involved in this deification of the Emperor, the "god makers" simply dipped into the deposit of Christian belief, applying our tenets to the Emperor, and attempting to justify their procedure by our canons of criticism. This official apology for the divinity of the Emperor was no mere academic tit-for-tat. To deny the major premise of the military's syllogism was tantamount to *lèse-majesté* during those years of crisis. The notorious "thought police" were quick to apprehend anyone whose convictions, religious or otherwise, did not jibe squarely with the official creed.

The government, principally for purposes of foreign consumption, maintained the fiction of religious freedom in Japan, but the fact is that the Japanese people were not free to accept Christianity to the exclusion of belief in the "divine Emperor" myth. As far as pure inward conviction was concerned, the military were content to let sleeping dogs lie; but in regard to the outward observances of the Emperor cult, especially in official life, they tolerated no heterodoxy. The civilian government was painfully embarrassed by the none-too-subtle intrigues of the military, in the latter's endeavor to wed the Japanese people, by religious ties if need be, to a "divine" Emperor, whose omnipotence was not his own to wield.

The intellectual confusion resulting from this campaign of deification was so profound as to make those who sponsored it ridiculous. The Japanese mind is anything but philosophical, and in the dither of theological speculation stirred up by the military, it was completely at a loss to penetrate such abstruse ideas as divinity, triunity, duality of nature, eternity, and the like. In fact, the very first of these several concepts was enough to halt the whole process of speculation. To even an educated Japanese, "divinity" is a very vague term. To him, it connotes a feeling, rather than a notion having definite philosophical or theological significance. In the Japanese mind, a god, or *kami,* really means only a superior type of being, which usually inhabits the spirit world.

Thus, not only the imperial ancestors, but the nation's historically great, are all "divinities"—Emperor Meiji, Admiral Togo, and, if Japan had emerged victorious from the recent war, Tojo and company. The Japanese, if the fever seized them, would not have the least hesitation about enshrining George Washington, Abraham Lincoln, and mayhap General MacArthur, as *kami.*

Indeed, a number of foreigners who perished in the great earthquake in 1923 were "deified" along with certain Japanese who lost their lives on that occasion. In short, it is easily possible, and altogether permissible, to evolve ever so many gods and goddesses out of the magic stuff of *kami*. And the Japanese have not been loath to do so throughout their long religious history, so that today they speak of their "myriad deities."

Consequently, the furore that ensued among foreigners over the Japanese Government's definition of the Emperor's "divinity" was really a tempest in a teapot, the vehemence of which was largely lost upon the Japanese. It was not so much the militarists' insistence upon the "divinity" of the Emperor, as their insidious attempt to interpret it as implying subordination of Christ, that brought grief to the Christians of Japan.

Apart from the difficulties growing out of the jingoes' endeavor to "Japanize" the Christian Faith, both Catholics and Protestants in Japan had other crosses to bear. As in every totalitarian country, the police in pre-war Japan were a law unto themselves. In league with the military, they regarded all Christian missioners as spies. Since the missioners were believed to be spies, patriotic Japanese were expected to have nothing to do with them. And woe to those who were suspected of "complicity with spies"—as were many catechists of Catholic churches. Manifold pressure was brought to bear on individual Catholics and Protestants in every walk of life. Not a few were dismissed from positions having only the slightest official connection, simply because they continued to attend churches that were, perforce, in the care of foreign missioners. In the neighborhood associations, into which the whole Empire had been divided, people who were more Christian than Japanese were distinctly in disfavor with their fellows.

Many a devout Christian was summoned to police headquarters during those trying years preceding World War II, to be accosted with such incriminating questions as: "Who is the greater, *Tenno* or Christ?" And it was not considered healthy to reply, as some compromisers tried to do, by putting other innocent questions, such as: "Which is more important, water or air?" The answer to these queries elaborated by experts in "thought control" often involved dire consequences, inasmuch as the police were prone to interpret even allegiance to God as *lèse-majesté*.

In their community relationships, too, Christians felt the heavy hand of oppression. The military, appealing ironically to the witness of the Bible, declared that the manifold divisions of the Christian Church were neither Christian nor desirable! With the simplicity of military efficiency, they proceeded to bang the heads of the Protestant denominations together, obliging the latter in 1941 to merge their several identities into one legal entity, known as the "United Church of Christ in Japan." The Anglican and Seventh Day Adventist Churches refused to join the union, but before long they found themselves in the embarrassing position of seeing their interests compulsorily administered by officers of the new corporation.

As for the Catholic Church, there was no alternative to recognizing it as a separate entity. Its stature was such as to discourage any ill-timed attempt to merge it with the other Christian denominations. The jingoes hoped eventually to whittle it down to the desired size, so they had no wish to be precipitate. For the present, they would be satisfied with obliging the foreign members of the Catholic hierarchy to resign in favor of Japanese, who were expected to prove more amenable.

In this labyrinth of variable oppression, no one was put to death, to the best of the author's knowledge. But multitudes of faithful souls were physically harried, mentally tortured, and socially ostracized. The Japanese, however, are a long-suffering people, accustomed to centuries of severe regimentation, to which they submit almost by second nature. In times of crisis, they find it easy to draw upon hidden reserves of fortitude, while squirming under the exactions of an oppressive regime. And this they do with a great deal of native ingenuity. For example, the late Prince Konoye was famous for his fits of migraine, which conveniently prevented him from attending sessions of the Diet whenever a clash was imminent. Similarly, Shinjiro Yamamoto, Japan's foremost Catholic, always was indisposed when he was invited to participate in the Shinto ceremonies conducted by the Emperor at the Imperial Sanctuary.

Such, in general, was the situation from 1936 to 1941, following the return of the samurai to power. Japanese Christians, undaunted by the stern realities that confronted them constantly, lived, like their fellow countrymen, in hopes of brighter days—days of release from the fears and tensions with which their lives were charged. Unfortunately, the situation on the religious front, as on all others, was destined to worsen before it could improve.

8. *War Comes to Otsu*

THE CRISIS, which everyone except the mad-dog militarists had been loath to conjecture, broke upon the international horizon with the attack on Pearl Harbor, December 7, 1941. To Americans at home, the war came as a stunning surprise. This should not have been the case, because the world situation was too clearly orientated toward war to warrant reliance on wishful thinking. To the American missioners stationed in Japan, the outbreak of hostilities was no surprise. Psychologically, the missioners had been prepared for the worst.

In this connection, the author can speak from first-hand experience, because he was one of those Americans who lived in Japan through the last hectic months preceding World War II.

After years of intimate contact with the Japanese people, we could sense their moods. Several months before the attack on Pearl Harbor, we felt, as if by some sixth sense, that Japan had despaired of a peaceful settlement of her difficulties with the West. Long before the thunderclap, Nippon had set her face toward war, as the world now knows. The volcano of secret military activity that began to seethe beneath the nation's apparently unperturbed exterior, fitted into that martial pattern like a hand in a glove. And the never-ending instances of galling and insupportable restrictions on the fundamental liberties of foreigners were all of a piece.

Without a written permit, seldom issued by the military police, foreigners, especially Americans, could no longer travel by rail to any point outside the city or county in which they resided. Foreigners were not allowed to telephone or telegraph in English. Their correspondence was censored more painstakingly than it had been during the preceding five years; consequently, a letter requiring less than a week for delivery within the limits of the city in which it was mailed was a rarity, indeed. Surveillance by uniformed police, as well as by men in civilian attire, was intensified tenfold. Domestic servants were suborned. In the case of missioners, members of their congregations were frequently grilled by the police about their pastor's affairs.

Ambassador Joseph C. Grew protested to the Japanese Government against this rampant discrimination, which affected American citizens in particular. The Ambassador's protest was in vain. No amelioration of the situation followed. On the contrary, things went from bad to worse.

In addition to experiencing personal inconveniences of all kinds, the missioners were seriously hampered in the work of the ministry. Detectives and military police appeared frequently in the churches to criticize the foreigner's sermons. These agents often intruded themselves into the homes of the faithful, interrogating the latter at will, and sometimes attempting to deter them from the practice of their religion by suasion or outright threats. To impugn the patriotism of Christians was the most common device of the police, whether civil or military.

In some places the police went so far as to try to stampede Japanese Catholics into attributing crimes of one kind or another to the local missioner. In one parish in Hokkaido—the northern island—hundreds of Catholics were summoned to police stations and grilled for hours, in a shameless attempt to jail the innocent young curate. The unfortunate pastor of the same church, a French-Canadian priest, had served two years of an unjust sentence before the author was repatriated in 1942. This was only one of the numerous and scandalous miscarriages of justice affecting foreigners in pre-war Japan.

During 1941, even before the war began, it was the easiest thing imaginable to get into a Japanese jail! Several months before the attack on Pearl Harbor, I was trying to assist an American missioner from Korea to secure the necessary permits to leave Japan; for a foreigner actually needed an assortment of official permissions, before he could return to his homeland. After a few days of haunting police stations, government offices, and so forth, we obtained the necessary permits. We went by trolley to the boat train; but at the terminal, in sight of hundreds of people, we were taken off the tram by an armed policeman. He paraded us through the streets, first to a police booth, then to the central police station. There we were detained until our would-be departant's train—the last to leave for Yokohama in time to catch the steamer for America— had pulled out. Then about midnight, we were "discovered" by an irate officer of the law, who accused us of invading the police station. Ejected forthwith, we considered ourselves fortunate not to have been entertained longer as "national guests."

At least six months before the outbreak of hostilities, an old French missioner in a southern diocese was jailed on suspicion of being a spy. The reason was that, one day when planes zoomed over his rectory, the old priest, thinking to jest with his Japanese housekeeper, had exclaimed: "Under the table, Auntie! Chiang Kai-shek's planes are overhead!" Auntie dutifully reported this bit of humor, and the missioner was remanded to jail for several weeks.

Earlier still, a South American clergyman, who was conducting a series of spiritual exercises at several churches in Japan, narrowly escaped imprisonment for unburdening himself of what he considered a joke. The poor man had been plagued everywhere he went by detectives and other police, who insisted that he fill out an elaborate questionnaire innumerable times. At last the clergyman would have no more of it; he countered by referring his questioners to the police station where he had been interviewed. But the detective concerned persisted in trying to get his own information.

When he came to the query, "What is your occupation?" the man of the cloth replied (facetiously, as he thought), "Oh, I'm an admiral of the Swiss Navy." "Ah, is that so?" replied the questioner, and he greedily noted down this important bit of information.

When, a few hours later, it was processed at headquarters, indignation reached a high pitch. "Why, Switzerland has no navy!" Evidently, the officials concluded, this individual who claimed to be a Swiss admiral was not even a gentleman, not to mention an admiral. On the contrary, he probably was a dangerous spy! Forthwith, a detective was assigned to shadow continuously the man from South America, until he left Nippon for more hospitable shores.

Whenever an incident of this kind (many of them occurred weekly) came to the attention of foreigners, it provided hilarious entertainment. The spy fever had reached such proportions that the police were making themselves ridiculous. The situation, shortly before the outbreak of the war, was really ludicrous, and yet it always had its tragic side. No foreigner could shake off the sense of impending disaster that weighed so heavily on everyone. Missioners could not undertake the most insignificant activity without the conscious fear that it was likely to be of no avail in a very short time.

At last, after months of gnawing tension, the bombshell burst. The Japanese military, arrogant because of earlier successes, were convinced of the "softness" of the white race. They had elected to gamble the fortunes of empire upon a single throw of the dice. The stakes were high, and the game was desperately played. But it was lost on that first jittery throw, when the Japanese forces failed to capitalize on the destruction inflicted upon the American position. The samurai, oblivious of *bushido*—the warrior's code that he long since had dishonored up and down the length of China—staggered the Westerner, but did not succeed in demoralizing him. On the contrary, Japan's initial successes temporarily demoralized her own subjects, leading many of them to think that the war had been won with the fall of Singapore.

The author can never forget that eventful day of December 7—it was December 8 in Japan—in 1941. About nine o'clock in the morning I was at work in an upper room. Suddenly I was conscious of the entry door sliding quietly in its groove; then I heard subdued voices. My housekeeper called up the stairs, a little quaver in her voice, "Spiritual Father, police to see you!"

As I went down, I remembered well how they had called at my home twice a day during the preceding week. In the entry I found Kinoshita San, a detective from the central police station. His hat was in his hand, and his swarthy face was like a prune—all puckered with suppressed excitement and importance. In funereal tones, he bade me not to think of leaving the house that day. Suspecting that this was only another of many arbitrary actions on the part of the local authorities, I requested an explanation. But my visitor would say nothing more, except to promise to return later in the day, when he would acquaint me with the reasons that prompted this prohibition.

True to his word, Kinoshita San returned within the hour. It was war, he said, and I must be prepared for many unpleasant experiences. Under no condition was I to leave the house. "The people of Otsu are very excitable," he warned, "and you might be mobbed by them."

I was inclined to give him the benefit of the doubt, because I remembered from a study of Japanese history that the last Czar of the Russians narrowly escaped assassination when, as crown prince, he visited this city years ago. Yes, home was the place for me. Besides, I had work to do, in blacking out my cottage in accordance with the directions of air-raid wardens, who suddenly appeared everywhere. Late that night, between one and two o'clock, I was awakened by what I thought was an altercation outside. A group of men approaching the house had been challenged by the guard posted at my gate. After a brief interchange of words, the newcomers began to hammer loudly on the door.

When the terrified housekeeper opened to them, they

thrust in a fellow missioner, with the peremptory order, "Put him up for the night!"

The missioner was my former companion, Brother Clement, who had been in a hospital in Kobe (about two hours away by train) for several weeks. Despite doctor's orders, the police insisted on bringing him back to his domicile in Shiga County. I made a bed for him, and bade him sleep—a thing impossible to do, with the jabbering of the guards downstairs, who evidently were as excited as ourselves.

Early next morning, the chief of the foreign section of the municipal police appeared at my home in full regalia. He told me that his country was at war with mine. At a signal from the man in gold braid, four or five detectives entered and proceeded to ransack the house from top to bottom. My camera, typewriter, radio, stationery, correspondence, personal files, church records—all were carried off. Every article of clothing not on my person was closely examined, especially at the seams. When the detectives had finished their official inspection, they left behind them a scene of indescribable confusion.

Early the same afternoon, Brother Clement and I were ordered to transfer our personal effects to the basement of the parish church. Rain was falling heavily, but that did not matter: the police were resolved that our place of internment should be ready by evening. For hours I shuttled back and forth between my little Japanese house and the church, straining under baggage, bedding, and such pieces of furniture as we were allowed to take. Police lined the route of this one-man caravan, standing under protecting umbrellas, but never offering to help bedraggled me. I tried to take a shred of comfort in the thought that somehow I was God's coolie; but I knew that not for God, but for America, had I come to such a pass.

In the church basement, my companion was putting things in order as fast as his weakened condition would permit. We placed our bedding on the mat-covered floor, arranged tables and chairs, and prayed for a stove to kill the damp chill that was already in the air. As we were surveying our monastic retreat, a delegation appeared on the scene. Mr. Van W., a Dutch citizen of our acquaintance, had arrived, in the company of a detail of police. No sooner had we arranged the few belongings of that elderly gentlemen, than the voices at the door announced the arrival of still another internee. This time it was a Maryknoll missioner, escorted by several detectives.

Shortly after we had spread Father Merfeld's pallet on the floor, in came Father Witte from Hikone, an hour away by train, with the inevitable escort of police. As one of the missioners later remarked: "You'd think they had the U. S. Army at bay, the way they surrounded me!"

The shades of night were falling fast by the time we

had put the finishing touches to Shiga County Concentration Camp. Fortunately, we were allowed out to take our meals, under guard, at my former residence. There at supper time I found my housekeeper, her morale badly shaken by the events of the day. She had done her best to provide dinner for the five internees, and it had been a new and trying experience for her, after having cooked so long for only one person.

Naturally, the housekeeper wished to discuss the situation with me, but the police would not allow it. They made plain the fact that she was no longer working for me. She was then and thereafter in the employ of the Japanese Government, although her salary and the running expenses of the house must be met by me for months to come. Back again we went to our subterranean keep, where we passed the night, tucked in by sergeant major, who sat at his desk keeping watch over the dangerous characters asleep beneath emergency floodlights.

Days passed—weeks, it seemed to us—filled with sleeping, walking, talking, shivering in the same room. Only the change of guards, and our brief excursions to my former home for meals, broke the monotony of those cheerless eternities. I can still remember how unhurriedly we walked the short distance between church and home. Never was air so fresh, and never was fresh air such a luxury. Even now, when my mind wanders back to those troubled days, I can almost feel the cool breeze that touched my cheek, as we paused there on the green heights above blue Lake Biwa.

One day, toward the end of the first week of our internment, the chief of the provincial police put in an appearance. Dressed in his best uniform, with gold braid and brass buttons gleaming in the faded sunlight, he burst into our narrow place of confinement. Two similarly uniformed assistants followed close at his heels. The little cavalcade drew up with a jerk, and there before us stood Mr. Asari, the picture of importance, leaning on his long, curved sword.

This dignitary was obviously carried away by the recent successes of the Japanese Army and Navy. Time and again he chuckled, "My, didn't Roosevelt make a mistake!"

Failing to appreciate Mr. Asari's enthusiasm, I proceeded to register a complaint, which irked that worthy not a little. "Was it according to international law," I demanded, "to shut us up in a cold, often damp, always ill-lighted, basement never intended for human habitation, without fresh air or space for exercise?" I complained, also, that two of our number were ill; and that a third, because of his age, might become so.

Mr. Asari impatiently heard me out, his face a mask of complete indifference and even boredom. His only reply was that if we were not satisfied with the basement of the church, he would confine us in the church proper. I tried to explain that the Catholics among us could never agree to inhabit the House of God, especially since there were many other more suitable places available. But the mask before me registered not the least interest in my appeal. Off on another tack, I suggested that we be interned in my former residence, especially since I was obliged to rent it for the convenience of the kitchen.

"If a kitchen is your worry," the mask replied, "I will have a hose run in here for water, and you can use a portable, charcoal stove for cooking." I could see that I was getting nowhere, so I said nothing more.

The chief's assistant, Mr. Arai, was obviously a fair-minded individual, but he had no authority in the presence of his superior. When the latter had brought the business of his visit to a satisfactory conclusion, he strode toward the door. Said Mr. Arai, as he met my eyes, "Of course, we intend to treat you people from the standpoint of humanity."

Said I, "I understand." With that, the little cavalcade swept out.

Later, the police decided to transfer us from the basement of the church to my residence across the street. There a formidable problem presented itself. How were we to provide living quarters for five adults in two rooms twelve-by-nine feet, and one room six-by-three feet, in size, on the second floor of a Japanese house? Three of our number volunteered to sleep on *futons*—thick quilts to be spread on the floor. During the day, these quilts are rolled up and put away. Nothing could be done about the furniture—we needed the things, although they encroached seriously upon our small preserve.

Running the length of the two rooms was a narrow, enclosed veranda. The windows of this veranda gave on a busy street, at the foot of a steep incline on which the house was built, and they seemed to enlarge our cramped estate. They were windows opening on the world of which we used to be a part! Downstairs were a kitchen, a tiny dining room, and a Japanese bath. The bath consisted of a stove surmounted by a small iron vat, into the sizzling waters of which we used to descend quite gingerly, and from which we ascended with the greatest alacrity. This crowded little house was the place of our sojourn for several months.

During the first two weeks, we did hardly more than huddle around the little barrel of fire that we called a stove, saying our prayers and discussing every subject under the sun, from the fate of our associates in other counties, to the birth of that new world which, we knew, must emerge from the crucible of World War II, if all the bloodshed were not to be in vain. The member of the group who was not a Catholic, no doubt found it hard to be locked up with a parcel of "Romans."

"But it might have been worse," poor Mr. Van W. used to say. "If our Protestant pastor had not returned to America, he, too, would have been interned in this Roman stronghold!" Sometimes the good Dutchman would look at us, sitting in a semicircle around the stove, and shake his head incredulously. "In Holland no one would ever take any of you young Americans for Dutch pastors. You are not solemn enough!"

In our situation it was difficult to be solemn. The house was so small that we were constantly tripping over one another. Again, we never knew what surprising dish might emerge from the culinary department. At the least suspicious sound, the guards would rush into our midst, with resulting embarrassment to all. The official diarist, too, kept watch on us, recording in his book of doom every item of our behavior. All this was a trifle hilarious; but we had, also, experiences that tasted of hardship.

One of our earliest crosses was the lack of fresh air. The police went so far as to seal the windows, and the guards never permitted us to go out of doors. When the inspector made his rounds to check the diary of our doings, which the guards kept with meticulous care, we used to torment him with requests for permission to go out in the air for exercise. But the authorities were deaf to our pleas, until we developed severe, sleep-destroying headaches from the fumes of charcoal fires that the guards kept alive in the house. Not until several weeks after our internment was our petition granted; and then we were allowed only thirty minutes daily in the yard, under the eye of an alert guard.

Time and time again, we despaired of the food problem. During the year before the outbreak of war, Japan had been suffering from scarcity of most of the foods that make up the foreigner's diet. The authorities, who were always niggardly in their dealings with us, soon decided that we should be put on the native diet of rice, fish, greens, and tea—a diet poor in proteins, to say the least. This sudden impoverishment of our table, coming as it did in the midst of winter, was not calculated to fortify our constitutions. We internees, however, were not the only ones who found the situation trying.

Never shall I forget the loyalty of my housekeeper, Mrs. T., the frail little woman who cooked our frugal meals. How much she suffered rather than betray her trust, we shall never know. But from things we heard, it was easy to imagine a little of what she went through. Ignoramuses carped at her for continuing in the employ of "enemy nationals." Super-patriots refused to sell, or sold grudgingly, the things that, in rain or shine, she trudged to purchase for us foreigners, who had not the slightest claim upon her benevolence. Among her friends, well-meaning people advised her to have done with an impossible situation; but Mrs. T. would not heed their advice. As conditions worsened, I feared that her health would yield to the strain of worry and overwork, and I advised her to resign; but she closed her ears to my suggestion.

Mrs. T.'s choice had not been easy to make. Because

of the persistent interference of the police and other local officials, she was hard-pressed in the practical management of Shiga County Concentration Camp. Often she used to weep at her work in the kitchen, overwhelmed by a sense of bewildered desolation. The hardships of the moment were bitter enough for Mrs. T., but her memories of the recent past were poignant ones, which swelled her grief.

She had seen the parish grow from a handful of Catholics, who worshiped in a renovated bakery, to a congregation of more than a hundred, having the largest and prettiest church in town. Now all was changed. Church and basement school were closed. There was no Presence in the church. Sunday Mass had been discontinued. The catechist, who had always been on hand to greet the faithful, languished in prison because he had whispered to me, as the police ransacked my house: "Spiritual Father, it is war! The bombs already are falling on Pearl Harbor." The parishioners were still being summoned to police stations, where they were cross-questioned sometimes for eight hours at a stretch.

Little Mrs. T.'s red eyes were eloquent of all these things. Now, as I go back in fancy to those days through which I seem to have lived only in dreams, I feel that we missioners received many a blessing because of the tears shed by that faithful little lady with the long, wide sleeves.

9. Priests and Prisons

THE POLICE HAD TAKEN every precaution to isolate us internees from the rest of the world. The day after war broke out, they had confiscated our radios, cameras, and typewriters. Although I was interned in my own home, the neighbors had been warned not to speak to me on the rare occasions when I might be allowed to leave the premises. How plainly I could read this in the eyes of the little children! Once happily familiar with "Mr. Foreigner," they silently scurried away at my approach under police guard. But in spite of the twenty-four-hour vigilance of the guards, I managed to maintain a minimum of contact with the outside world by means of the "bamboo wireless."

Thus it was that I learned how ailing Magdalena K.'s young daughter had been summoned from her switchboard in the telephone exchange, to be questioned by the police because she had attended a church in charge of an "alien spy." I could well understand with what embarrassment this Korean girl would have to face her Japanese companions thereafter.

By "bamboo wireless" I heard, also, how old Anna U. had confounded her judges, on the winter night when she was grilled by the jingo police. They were questioning her about the American missioner.

"Don't you know, Ancient One, that this man is an enemy of our Nippon—a spy?"

"I am sorry to be rude, sir," answered old Anna, "but I know nothing of the kind."

"He is an American. I repeat: an American!"

"I never adverted to that fact, sir. I know him only as a man of God."

The detectives took another tack: "But surely you know, madame, that your Catholic church was built with American money. Everything in it came from America!"

Old Anna listened patiently, her withered hands crossed in her wide kimono sleeves. Her voice was unruffled as she replied, a little quizzically:

"I dare say, sir, that the God in our Church of St. Mary's of the Lake didn't come from America. The God of Christians is not like the *kami* of Japan. He is not the God of any single nation. It is not true, therefore, to say that we Christians worship an American God. Heaven's Lord is God of all mankind, sir."

All around her, hostile eyes glinted angrily. Then the senior officer, clearly worsted by the silken flow of old Anna's eloquence, irritably motioned her out into the night. And the night was no longer dark, for Anna had been privileged to play the role of a confessor of the Faith.

The spark of her samurai strain still burned in the old lady's breast. Proudly she used to recount the story of her grandfather's conversion to the Catholic Faith, when we gathered after Sunday Mass to sip green tea. The tale ran like this:

"Grandfather had a great dislike for all preachers of religion. In his eyes, they were merely hypocrites. There was not a bonze or a Shinto priest in Shiga County whom he had not bearded in the sanctuary.

"One day he challenged a Shinto priest who had just reminded his congregation that 'Mr. God' reposed within the tabernacle of his shrine. 'I dare you, sir!' roared Grandfather, 'to open yon holy house in proof of your statement that Mr. God resides there.'

"The pagan priest was enraged by this irreverent request. He flung open the tabernacle door—and exposed to his own horrified gaze and that of his congregation a monstrous serpent, coiled up in that woodland shrine.

"This was too much for Grandfather. Over the hills to Kyoto, he stamped in a smoldering rage, eager to sample the wares of the foreign missioner in the Lord of Heaven Church.

"Famous Father Villion was absent when Grandfather arrived at the rectory. The housekeeper—Mrs. Middle Ricefield, her name was—offered Grandfather a chair, bidding him hang his hips. You know, Spiritual Father, that is what sitting on a foreign chair looks like to us —hanging the hips.

"Well, it wasn't long before the old chair collapsed

under Grandfather's weight. In a heap on the floor, he surveyed the offending piece of furniture, remarking in disgust how its shaky legs had been wired together. Grandfather stormed, 'What kind of person can this foreigner be, in whose house I find such junk?'

"The priest's faithful housekeeper was indignant. 'The Spiritual Father is a poor man! The little money he receives from his native France, he spends on poor Japanese people. He can't afford fine furniture! Besides, sir, what has fine furniture to do with religion?'

"Soon Father Villion returned, and Grandfather was not long in discovering the mettle of that Spiritual Father. Grandfather went home a Christian. In his forthright way, he immediately carried the family shrine into the street and set it on fire, in full view of our horrified neighbors. Grandfather was a terror!"

The "bamboo wireless" told me, too, how in a parish in the northwest of Japan, seven members of a small congregation were jailed for loyalty to their Faith. Two of them were young mothers, who had been torn from their little children. During sixteen months of imprisonment, they were not influenced by cold, hunger, and threats. One of the women was condemned to solitary confinement, because she refused to tread upon a crucifix.

The "crime" for which these courageous Japanese were imprisoned may be gleaned from the record (if it has not already been destroyed) of the proceedings against Agnes N., who bore glorious witness to her Faith. States the official account: "She emphatically declared that there is only one true God, and that all other gods are nothing more than idols, and therefore should not be worshiped . . . the Emperor of Japan is not divine."

These are only a few of the examples of Christian faith and fortitude on the part of Japanese men and women, which might be cited here. Suffice it to say that, up and down the length of Nippon, there were noble souls—our brethren in the Faith—who clung to their religion in spite of persecution of every kind.

During the ten years preceding the outbreak of World War II, the Catholic Church, in common with other Christian denominations, had been subjected to sporadic persecution of varying intensity. The Tokyo officials were eloquent with protestations of friendship toward the Catholic Church, but the fact that the government permitted those ever-recurring attacks against the Christian religion belied its expressed policy of toleration. The truth of the matter is that genuine, vibrant, red-blooded Christianity—not the emasculated, part-pagan compromise that too many cowardly individuals were willing to accept—could not co-exist with Shinto, the crusading quasi-religion of the militarists of Japan.

When, therefore, the jingoes were well settled in the saddle after the outbreak of war, they promptly showed their true colors. Churches were closed or confiscated; foreign missioners as well as native ecclesiastics were shamelessly abused; the faithful were oppressed with all the ingenuity madmen could devise. The lurid tale of frantic search, endless cross-questioning, grim imprisonment, and outright cruelty, which seeped across the "bamboo wireless," was sickening. And all that woe had befallen innocent, law-abiding men and women, simply because they worshiped God according to their lights. History repeats itself: in modern Japan, Christians were persecuted for their Faith just as their ancestors had been oppressed centuries earlier.

As months wore on, it occurred to the Home Office in Tokyo that some of the Japanese concentration camps might not be up to standard. Consequently, representatives were sent to inspect the various houses of detention. The official who inspected our crowded quarters agreed that some measure of amelioration was imperative. We had never ceased to complain about the insufficiency of the space allotted to us. True, Mr. Van W. had been permitted to return to his Japanese family, but the other internees were still treading on one another's toes in their unbelievably tiny quarters.

The local police reacted to the directive of the official from the Home Office, with the proposal to transfer us to a centuries-old Buddhist temple. We suggested that a Buddhist temple might be an inappropriate place in which to intern Catholic priests. But the authorities thought not—unless we objected to rats or spooks— because bonzes there were none. When we asked if the

authorities could not find a decent, six-room house in a
city of eighty thousand people, they admitted that there
were many such places, but they did not intend to rent
one for us.

"Buddhist temple or not, you are being much better
treated than our nationals are treated in the United
States!" one officer declared. Such was the apparently
sincere conviction of those misinformed puppets of the
ruling clique.

They and their fellows were absolutely sure that
whatever a Japanese does, no matter in what department
of human endeavor, is infinitely nobler and far superior
to anything anyone else might essay. If the undoing of
Japan can be ascribed to any single factor, I daresay
that that factor is a morbid mental condition best diagnosed as the psychological blind-spot.

Early in March of 1942, the Home Office decided to
transfer the internees of Shiga County to the "Second
Detention House" in Kobe, a city a short distance from
our place in Otsu. The day before our departure was
spent in drawing up legal instruments to "guarantee dis-
position" of all property other than our personal effects.
We were allowed two pieces of luggage for each internee
—a trunk and a suitcase. Being in his own home, the
author was able to cram everything needful into his
baggage; but the other internees were less fortunate, all
of them having great difficulty in packing a necessary
minimum of their belongings. Everything was examined

by the local police as with a fine-toothed comb, before
we were permitted to pack.

The author remembers an amusing incident in connection with that long, exhausting session.

The little American flag that I had treasured through
the long years since I left home, caught the attention
of the police official who was inspecting my baggage.
I had declared it simply as "one flag." Now came the
police interrogation.

"What flag?" the official demanded. "My country's
flag," I replied, my heart fit to burst with pride. "Open
it!" the other commanded.

In Japan anything sacred—such as an Imperial Re-
script, for example—is unrolled with the greatest ceremony. That little flag with the stars and stripes was
never so sacred as then. I had wrapped it in a new hand-
kerchief of white Korean silk, and secured it with a
narrow red ribbon.

"This will take time," I said, beginning to unroll the
silken wrapper. "This is very precious to me," I added.
"Oh, it is, is it?" answered the officer, a note of sarcasm
in his voice.

Very deliberately, and with all the outward show of
inward reverence suited to the occasion, the little banner
was unrolled. A moment of silence followed. Then the
guard, a country bumpkin, exclaimed, "Mm, it's an interesting flag."

But the days of complimenting foreigners had passed,

and the police official crisply interposed: "All right! What else?"

The little flag, however, had to be carefully rewrapped before our business could proceed. The minions of the law openly betrayed their impatience at this leisurely demonstration of sentiment.

Toward evening, I ventured into the kitchen to present my faithful housekeeper with a small monetary gift. As I stood speaking to her by means of signs, there came a scratching on the window pane. Then the door slipped silently in its groove, admitting old Magdalena K. and Maria S., both Koreans. They had come "to make honorable parting."

As they huddled in a corner, crowding the charcoal and firewood, Magdalena whispered in her broken Japanese: "Maria says that she is going to the heavenly country soon. She wishes to look upon the Spiritual Father's honorable countenance before she disappears."

The old lady stood there in her flowing white silks, bowing and murmuring something in the language of her ancestors—that forbidden Korean tongue, which the Japanese military were trying to extirpate in one of the greatest cultural oppressions of all time. She was running her wrinkled hands over her wizened face, signifying something that both of us could understand, but neither of us could express in language. Then the guard began to stir on the other side of the paper screen, and my callers melted into the twilight.

Early on the morrow, our police escort appeared. As I stood at the door, looking across the fields to my church of St. Mary's of the Lake, a monument to the best ten years of my life, an irritable guard broke in on my reverie. "April first! But no April fool! Let's go!"

My housekeeper, Mrs. T., and her two little daughters were on hand to accompany me to the railroad station; at their mother's behest, the girls had come from their school in distant Akita, to bid me a last farewell. The "bamboo wireless" had been working again. As our unimposing procession wended its way to the depot, many a window framed a sympathetic face. We were not running the gantlet. Far from it! We were in a procession watched by our friends.

The train pulled in. The three bright butterflies on the platform bowed and said, "*Sayonara*—if it must be so."

Two hours later our group of internees arrived in Kobe. After a short tram ride and a shorter walk, we came to a long, two-story, barrack-like building on a steep hill. There was a blatant swastica painted on its gate. A suspicion crossed our minds: were we to be interned under Nazi supervision? That would be the last straw! Fortunately, the swastica turned out to be Buddha's prayer wheel.

We made our way through mountains of bedding and baggage, to a small room called the "isolation ward" because speaking there was forbidden. In the "isolation ward," the Shiga police officially transferred us to the custody of the Kobe police.

Our new place of internment was known as the Eastern Lodge. It was an unpretentious hotel originally established for the convenience of the Parsee residents of Kobe. The wooden building was of cheap construction; it contained about forty private rooms, most of which could accommodate three persons. To the left of the entry, was a large dining room; to the right, a vegetarian dining room, about the size of a private room. The latter was used also as a reception room, and the internees jokingly referred to it as the "isolation ward."

A carpeted stairway led from the entry to the second floor. At the head of this stairway was the guard room, which overlooked the miniature garden and the sole avenue of approach. The building had electric light, but no provision for heating. In each bedroom there was a washstand, and at the far end of each floor there was a shower bath with the luxury of hot water. What a pleasing contrast to the provision in Otsu—the little iron vat, into which the five of us used to descend in order of sprightliness!

As the Eastern Lodge, the building was still nominally in the hands of its Indian owner, kindly Mr. Shroff. But as the Second Detention House, it was in the care of Mr. Ee, a friendly old Japanese who was a retired police sergeant. Recalled to active service, Mr. Ee had made the Eastern Lodge the best internment camp in

Kobe, if not in Japan. In addition to being superintendent of the Second Detention House, Mr. Ee was also a Shinto priest, and he acquitted himself of pastoral duties over the week ends.

This kindly old gentleman, whose perfectly bald head shone like burnished copper, entered the "isolation ward" soon after we arrived and inquired, "Who speaks Japanese?" When we told him that all of us could amble along in his mother tongue, he fairly beamed.

Mr. Ee made several attempts to memorize our names, but gave it up as an impossible job. Taking a room list from his pocket, he assigned the priests, two by two, to rooms on the ground floor. But when he came to Brother Clement, he looked closely at that Maryknoller's necktie; then he said, with an air of finality, "Since your religion is different, you will please share Mr. X.'s room on the second floor."

Poor Brother Clement! His companion turned out to be an Englishman, who was engrossed in Buddhism to the extent of denying the reality of the objective world. That night Brother laid his weary head to rest in an atmosphere of musty tomes bulging with Chinese characters. Before dozing off Brother ventured to ask, "Mr. X., how did you happen to become interested in Buddhism?"

A deep voice replied from the other side of the darkened room, "The same way you became interested in Christianity—by prenatal influence."

Said Brother Clement to us, on the morrow: "I asked no more questions. That nugget was too much for me!"

Long before December 8, business conditions had so thoroughly deteriorated that the majority of Indian merchants retired from Japan. Only sixty out of several hundred remained, and many of these intended to return to India as soon as they could liquidate their stocks. A mere handful of guests patronized the Eastern Lodge, and the manager was on the point of closing his establishment when the Japanese Government requisitioned it for a concentration camp.

The building was in a run-down condition at that time; but the first batch of internees, eager to make their surroundings as homelike as possible, soon improved it. They cleaned and fumigated most of the rooms and, in not a few cases, wholly or partially refurnished them with the help of Mr. Shroff. They had given the rooms assigned to us a preliminary cleaning, but it required days of devoted scrubbing before we were fully satisfied with our new quarters.

When our Shiga delegation arrived on the scene, there were about thirty-five internees already housed in the Eastern Lodge. Eight of them were Catholic missioners: a Belgian priest; a Canadian priest; and six Maryknollers —from Kyoto, Nara, and Tsu. The other internees comprised the following: ten Dutch citizens; about a dozen Americans, of whom five were Navy nurses from Guam; several British subjects; two Guatemalans; and

one Australian. There were also about six non-internees
—Indian boarders, whom the authorities had allowed to
remain in the hotel on condition that they would not
associate with the internees. As time went on the enrollment swelled to forty-five—a goodly houseful.

There was an admirable spirit of sympathy and cam-
araderie among the members of this heterogeneous community. No matter what a man's nationality or creed
might be, he was a brother internee, animated by similar
ideals and hopes and imprisoned for the same cause.
When the pioneers heard that twelve Catholic priests
would be interned with them, they were ready to swoon
at the thought of such an inundation of kill-joys. But
on the occasion of the farewell supper given us by Mr.
Shroff, proprietor of the Eastern Lodge, our non-Catholic companions generously admitted that the American
priests had done more to enliven the atmosphere and
make the situation tolerable than had any other single
group.

Soon after our arrival, we learned with relief that the
Second Detention House was a kind of little democracy
within an airtight oligarchy. The police were in charge
of the camp, and left us in no doubt on that point.
But within certain limits, they entrusted the general
discipline to the internees and allowed us to make sug-
gestions and initiate community reforms. In this ad-
visory capacity, the pioneers had elected a president and
two vice-presidents, who maintained contact with the

authorities and the internees. This proved to be a smooth working-arrangement, and remarkably little friction or misunderstanding marred our humdrum existence during the next three months. How different was this gentlemanly, almost friendly, regime from the uncivil, suspicious, puerile attitude of the Shiga County police!

The horarium of the day was simple: rising—6:30 A.M.; roll call and breakfast—7:15; roll call and lunch —12:30 P.M.; tea—4:00; roll call and dinner—7:30; roll call—9:00; lights out—9:30. We priests rose earlier than our fellow internees, in order to say Mass; for the rest of the day, the schedule was elastic enough to allow plenty of time for our breviary and studies. Mr. Shroff owned a near-by club, which he had maintained in the interests of the Parsee residents of Kobe. He and his Indian associates graciously arranged their activities so as to leave the club vacant for our use between two and four o'clock every afternoon. The internees were divided into two groups, who went "clubbing" on alternate days.

Mr. Ee kindly permitted us to say Mass publicly on Sundays, in a large room on the second floor of the club building. We took turns singing High Mass and preaching the sermon. The arrangement gave us splendid opportunity for a profession of faith, and also made it possible for our few lay Catholic companions to assist at the Holy Sacrifice. By the time our evacuation date arrived, the majority of our non-Catholic fellows had been to Mass at least once, and a few of them were regular attendants. One Sunday, just to assure himself that we were not "putting anything over" on him, Mr. Ee confided his temple to a substitute and very innocently appeared at Mass. He inquired about the subject matter of the sermon and, unlike the Shiga County police, he believed us when we told him the facts.

We have all heard that an army marches on its stomach. Internees, to be sure, are not army personnel, but they often have to put in their stint at marching, so they appreciate a good "mess." The little, glass-topped tables in the dining room of the Second Detention House never groaned under a goodly banquet, but they supported a consistently good menu calculated to carry the diners through many a hectic day. The Eastern Lodge had access to the markets of Kobe, and in some instances was a preferred customer. Moreover, the Kobe police were always willing to co-operate in regard to food supplies, and a trained hotel staff knew how to tide over deficiencies by many a culinary "miracle." Credit to whom credit is due: apart from an occasional excess of starches, the table at Second Detention House was good.

Here, as in Otsu, lack of exercise was the cause of universal lament. The garden between the hotel and the clubhouse was of the miniature type, with narrow, brick walks. (These walks had been laid out by the pioneer internees, and, though the police knew it not,

they formed the Union Jack, the letter W for Wilhel-
mina, and V for victory.) Consequently, we had almost
no place to stretch our legs. But the air was good, and
plentiful if too many did not try to inhale at the same
time. Mr. Ee recognized the need, and did his utmost to
arrange for all-day walks once or twice a month.

I remember well the first hike. We assembled in the
garden, with lunches under our arms, and the roll was
called two or three times. Lined up at last like a lot of
school children—the men first (Japan is a man's country), the ladies in the rear—we set out, with Mr. Ee
and his plainclothes assistants at the head, sides, and rear
of the column. Naturally, the tramp-tramp of forty
internees on a macadam road attracted attention, but
the Japanese we met were civil. For the most part, they
regarded us in silence as we passed by.

Now and then, however, the incurably curious dis-
cussed the situation in undertones: "Is that fellow over
there an American or an Englishman?" "How can you
tell the Dutch from the English?" "They all look alike,
but they are really as different as day and night." Then
a figure cruised by on a bicycle, and his quiet voice
reached our ears above the din of traffic: "Spiritual
Fathers, I am sorry for you."

As one might expect in the case of men long immured
in restricted quarters, there were a few casualties after
the first all-day walk. Old Mr. K. of Holland complained that he had a kink in his back. Mr. P., our genial

friend from Australia, reported that he felt "a pine in me laig." Even some of the young blades moved in a gingerly way, and the community was duly impressed with the hazards of a sudden transition from terra cotta to terra firma. Still, in spite of the crop of weary limbs and creaky joints, no one would consider foregoing the glorious liberty of the next excursion.

It is a fact of daily observation that men, beholding the same scene through the multicolored lens of circumstance, often react in diametrically opposite ways. What one despises as sheerest misfortune, another esteems as a most enviable lot. So it was in our small world of woe. We in the concentration camp writhed under numerous restrictions upon our normal liberty, and some regarded those checks as hateful fetters forged in the fiery smithy of the devil himself. But later arrivals who straggled in, singly or in pairs—poor wretches who had been fastened by gyves of steel to the dark floors of filthy prison cells —saw only the delectable abandon of respectable people temporarily detained in plebeian quarters, until the shadow of a worse evil should have passed.

10. Days of Detention

FROM THE CASE HISTORIES of the latecomers, we of the Eastern Lodge were able to piece out the story of December 8 in Kobe. As happened everywhere else in Japan, foreigners who had long been known to the local police as law-abiding persons were suddenly regarded, and treated, as the worst criminals. Police appeared without warning, and carried men away to internment camps or common jails. Many a father who left his home under police escort was not seen again by his dear ones until months later, when criminals in chrysanthemum-crested uniforms had arbitrarily convicted him of fancied violations of law, ranging from professional espionage to the accidental and incidental notice of such facts as could not escape the observation of even a moron. Nor were "spiritual fathers" spared: none of the French missioners in Kobe were seized; but in other parts of Japan, American, Canadian, English, and Belgian mission workers—Catholic and Protestant—fared ill.

From the new arrivals we learned that in some cases —for example, in Yokohama—the internment camps were little better than prisons. Men were crowded into close quarters in barrack-like structures, without heat to kill the damp winter chill. Food was insufficient, and it was served digustingly unprepared. Little provision was made for personal cleanliness. How general these conditions were, it is difficult to ascertain. The author feels that it would be unfair to generalize and condemn all Japanese internment camps as utter sinks of despair, but the Eastern Lodge certainly was a shining exception to the general run of them.

As a people, the Japanese had a low standard of personal comfort. Moreover, the Tokyo Government made the mistake of entrusting the internment of foreigners to local authorities, few of whom were men of intellectual caliber sufficient to handle a situation for which Japan had no precedent. To the best of the author's knowledge, international law never envisaged the imprisonment of nationals having a high standard of living, by people whose standards are appreciably lower. Be that as it may, there was the greatest discrepancy between the standards of internment camps in Nippon and those in the United States.

About Japanese prisons the author need say little. Many innocent foreigners who were straitened and encompassed in those vile keeps have already told the story of their experiences. Dark, unventilated, freezing holes, six feet by six, with no furniture except a roll of bedding and a length of straw matting on the concrete floor—such were the forbidding vaults that swallowed up many respectable, law-abiding, cultured people, without regard to sex, age, or health. Their diet was a bowl of soup, a single dish of rice moistened with green tea, and occasional vegetables. The food was shoved through a slot in the cell door, three times a day. The prisoners squatted in Japanese style, on the hard, cold floor, for eight or ten hours at a time, while doing the forced labor assigned by the prison authorities. The only distraction from that maddening eternity of unmerited entombment came once a day, when guards conducted the victims to a courtyard for an hour's exercise.

Adversity often brings out the noblest sentiments of the human heart. This is true of those who suffer, and also of those who witness the suffering. An illustration of this truth is the story of Doctor M.

An old gentleman of seventy, Doctor M., whom the author is privileged to count among his friends, had devoted the best years of his life to educating the youth of Japan. He was sentenced to two years of imprisonment in a "tomb" such as the author has described, because he had innocently shown to some acquaintance a letter from one of his former pupils, then a soldier on the China front. If the missive had contained any information likely to harm the Japanese aggressions, the blame should have fallen on the army censors, and not on innocent people at the receiving end of the line. Of course, there was not an iota of valuable information in Doctor M.'s letter. But it served a police officer as an excuse to repay an ancient grudge; or worse, as an excuse to bludgeon the elderly gentleman into admitting crimes that he had never even thought of committing. In reward for securing such an admission, the officer could obtain a degree of promotion.

So the aged, white-haired, American educator went to prison, leaving alone his ailing, palsied wife, who was nearly seventy years old. On Christmas Eve, the aged prisoner's tired mind harked back, not to his distant boyhood or his American home, but to One who, though infinitely great, had been born in circumstances worse than his, on the first Christmas, centuries ago. And that thought, like the touch of a phantom finger on a lyre, waked the music in the old man's unslumbering soul. He broke into a carol, whistling (for it was forbidden to sing in those bleak halls) the familiar notes that he had learned when a child. As he warmed to his role of troubadour, his heart seemed fit to burst with joy; like a long-caged bird suddenly set free, he trilled and warbled the sacred lays one after another, hardly pausing for breath.

On the morrow men would brush against him in the courtyard and whisper in a strange tongue, "Thank you for the concert last night." Before that, however, a guard stormed into his cell and struck the bard of Christ twenty times across the face. But then another guard stole down the corridor, softly opened the slot in the door, and shoved in a slice of jam-coated bread.

Thinking of that second Japanese guard, who was sent to prison because he had been kind to an American troubadour of Christ, the author penned the following paragraphs aboard the exchange ship, *Asama Maru*, as he was returning to the United States. Now, six years later, his sentiments have undergone no change.

"Our struggle in relation to Japan is, I think, against a system, not against a people. We are striking back at a thoroughgoing militarism which has so long brutalized the Japanese people themselves that in cases too numerous to mention their sense of humanity and decency has been blunted beyond all hope of cure. We are, naturally speaking, largely the product of our age, creatures of a regime, and it is a mystery to me how anyone born under the star of a hypocritical, unscrupulous, mystically rabid, almost frenetic militarism can manifest the lofty virtues we admire in so many Japanese. The existence of such illustrious exceptions, or (shall I say?) such exceptional examples, only goes to prove that the Japanese people, as such, are not bad. They are victims of a bad government which incidentally is not to be identified with their mythically divine, but actually very human, and presently very helpless Emperor, but with a vicious clique of militarists in boots and spurs who pervert their naturally good instincts by enlisting them for an unworthy cause. Not until these harpies go down to the doom which they have prepared for others, will the Japanese be free of the germ that fires their blood and the humor that harries their brain.

"When a man is unhinged, though he perpetrates the

most extraordinary feats of wickedness, we make allowances. We say that the poor fellow is not in his right mind, implying that if he were normal he would never dream of committing those excesses. Similarly in the case of Japan, I think we must ascribe the sometimes incredibly ludicrous, sometimes incredibly cruel episodes that occurred after December 8, to a country momentarily crazed by the rabies of militarism. No decent Japanese would condone, for example, the summary jailing on charges of espionage of a young lady schoolteacher, an American Protestant missionary, simply because she asked her pupils, by way of illustrating the superlative degree of adjectives, such questions as the following: 'What is the highest mountain in Japan?' 'What is the longest river in Japan?' Much less would such a Japanese excuse the barbarous 'water treatment,' in administering which the police used to tie up their victim into a ball, and force water—bucketful after bucketful—into his mouth and nostrils, until he lapsed into unconsciousness. When a man is sick, he isn't well; and when a nation goes berserk, it isn't sane."

At the Eastern Lodge, we found that later arrivals from other internment camps were overwrought and underweight. Those released from prisons, upon the demand of the American Government transmitted through the Swiss Legation in Tokyo, were gaunt and emaciated, almost invariably suffering from some ailment contracted or aggravated during their confinement. The advent of every one of those poor men was like the return of a long-lost brother. Once they had assured themselves about our loyalty, they told everything, talking with little let-up for three, four, five days at a time. We knew that they would never be normal again, unless they could rid their minds of the haunting nightmare through which they had lived. The author little appreciated what a scourge the memory of such a sufferer must have been, until he was awakened one night on the evacuation ship by the cries of a young man pleading in his sleep, "Don't kill me!" As a civilian, the young man had been through the siege of Hong Kong.

The arrival of a newcomer in our small community was an event akin to the birth of a baby in an ordinary family. Needless to say, our new comrades did not appear every day; but by the time talk of evacuation had progressed from the impossible to the probable stage, our quarters were full to overflowing. In such an expanding universe, peopled by such denizens with such pasts, conversation never lagged. Patriotism was at a white heat, and every battle was fought and refought with the seriousness of death.

We were convinced that the Allied Nations could not possibly have piled up the mountains of defeat credited to them by the *Osaka Daily*, which in our eyes was the most disreputable of propaganda sheets. The Allies would win! We were confident of victory—not because we had been prepared for this onslaught, and not because we were by natural endowment a superior race destined to win—but simply because in this hour of flux we represented the inalienable rights of man. We were Christian enough to recognize our past mistakes, and to resolve that a better world would issue from the crucible of this war of wars.

Still, there were those who wondered, those who faltered in this faith of the majority. They were men who had left their homes—little countries in Europe or Central America, which offered poor prospects to not especially talented people like themselves—and had gone to the far Orient as youths. They had grubbed for years to ensure the modest security that they enjoyed before December 8. They knew only the potentiality of the country that had harbored them, only the caliber of the people who had befriended them. In view of Japan's phenomenal martial successes, it seemed to such internees that the war must end in failure for the Allies. At best, if Japan did not win, the outcome would be a stalemate. Their knowledge was too circumscribed to let them see the vision of young America on wings. After the Japanese Navy had crippled our Pacific Fleet and had taken our bases in Guam and Wake, the doubters thought it extravagant fancy to say that one day Americans would span the deep and hover over those distant isles like angry birds of prey.

Hans D. was one of those young men who were not

sanguine over the prospects of an Allied victory. "I'm keeping my fingers crossed," he said, as we sat in the garden, enjoying the friendly rays of the April sun. "It's a big hop for any bird, especially when he has no place to stop and scratch his wings. I'm afraid your American eagles will never come," he jibed good-naturedly.

"They'll come. Never doubt it!" I rejoined. But at the same time, I was wondering impatiently why they had not come long ago. And then, after the doubter had departed, I soliloquized: "If I were over there in Washington, I'd show them how to conduct this war—I and my little flag! Oh, why don't they come? If only to cheer us who keep faith with them—"

I thought that my imagination was getting the better of me, for almost at that very moment, in the strangest coincidence of my life, I heard the drone of a powerful motor approaching from a distance. An American eagle had come! A big, streamlined plane roared into view, flying low over the stretch of railroad, only a rifle-shot away. I knew, as if by telepathy, that the brave men in that great, silver, fish-like bird heading toward the sea were of my race, and I was thrilled to the core of my being. As I learned later, this plane was one of General Doolittle's raiding party that had taken off from the deck of a carrier in the Pacific, and after spending those memorable "sixty seconds over Tokyo," had headed for secret landing fields in China.

According to next morning's newspapers, the day had

been hectic. American planes had been over Japan, the papers admitted; but they claimed (without too much attention to their mathematics) that Nippon's invincible air force had succeeded in shooting down eleven out of ten. However, it was evident that Japan's spell of security had been broken: the foreigner had invaded the land of the gods. A tremor of secret fear ran through the nation. If the eagle could come once, he could come again.

What other emotions stirred in the breasts of the people, we did not know, but we could guess. From then on, every night, our quarters were blacked out. We were forbidden to be out of doors during an air-raid alarm; forbidden, too, to look from the windows at passing planes. Guns were readied in the guard room, and the officer of the day changed from civilian dress to uniform. Rumors swept through the camp that, if the bombings were continued, we should be removed to the countryside.

But a more desirable transfer had been arranged. After months of negotiation, the American and Japanese Governments had agreed to an exchange of their interned nationals. The American Government was said to have demanded that Japan evacuate, also, all citizens of the United States who had been imprisoned after December 8, 1941.

Among the interned Catholic missioners, a doubt was raised about the advisability of their participation in the proposed repatriation. Were they free to leave Japan without specific orders to this effect? The doubt was referred to the Japanese ordinaries, who took the matter under advisement at a meeting in Tokyo. The Japanese hierarchy in turn referred the matter to the Holy See, through the Apostolic Delegate, Archbishop Paul Marella; and they submitted their own recommendation, that the missioners who were imprisoned or interned should be left free to take advantage of the exchange. The Holy See concurred in this recommendation. Thus Catholic missioners, who had remained at their posts in spite of repeated invitations by the American consuls to return to the United States, were enrolled among the prospective repatriates.

In continued confinement, the missioners would be able to do nothing except ruin their health. At liberty in their own country, they would be able to volunteer for service in other sectors of the Master's vineyard. As a matter of fact, the majority of Maryknoll missioners who returned to the United States from Manchuria, Korea, and Japan were assigned to other mission work in Central and South America a few months after their home-coming. In this way a group of static internees became a mobile unit in the great missionary army of the Catholic Church.

The proposed departure of the internees from Japan was scheduled for the middle of June, 1942. Until then, the days of our detention lengthened into ages.

11. Exiled to Home

THE DAY OF PARTING—June 16—dawned fair and balmy. We Americans had sent out what baggage the officials allowed us to take—one trunk and one suitcase, each—a week ahead, and we were unencumbered except for small hand luggage, out of which we had been living during the interim. At four o'clock in the afternoon, we made the rounds of the Eastern Lodge, shaking hands with the congenial companions of our exile. Some of them were hoping to be evacuated a month later, on the British exchange ship; others, for various reasons, expected to remain behind and see the grim struggle through to the bitter end.

The leave-taking was a little hard on all concerned. The members of the hotel staff were visibly affected. The whole community followed us to the gate that led to liberty—police, internees, hotel staff. Members of the Parsee Club waved to us from the windows of the building next door. Then we were out on the street. Good-by, England, Belgium, Holland, Canada, Central America, Australia, India! and *sayonara*, Japan!

The railroad station was alive with other contingents of American evacuees. In one spot was the group from Manchuria; in another place, those from Korea; and near by, those from central Japan. The delegation from

the south had gone ahead, and was waiting in Yokohama. When the last roll call was completed, and the
fact duly noted as usual that there had been no escapes,
we boarded the evacuation train.

Twilight deepened into night, as we pulled out of
Kobe. At ten the next morning, our train reached
Tokyo. We were conducted to the Station Hotel, where
the Japanese Government had provided a farewell lunch.
Tired after the long night's ride in day coaches, we were
glad to relax before negotiating the formalities of em-
barkation. At three o'clock in the afternoon, we en-
trained again for Yokohama, arriving at the pier less
than a half hour later.

After interminable checking and rechecking, we
boarded the *Asama Maru* and heaved an herculean sigh
of relief, thinking that soon we should be homeward
bound. But days passed—and still we lay at anchor in
the harbor. There were many conjectures about the delayed departure of the *Asama Maru,* but no definite
information. As the days lengthened into a week, we
began to fear that the evacuation would not materialize,
and some of the passengers made no secret of their in-
tention to commit suicide rather than return to internment or imprisonment in the land of the gods. When
the tension was at its height, suddenly, at one o'clock
in the morning on June 25, the good ship quivered and
slowly moved out to sea.

We numbered about a thousand passengers, and needless to say, accommodations were insufficient. At the insistence of Ambassador Grew, women and children were given the preferred quarters—and luckily for them! It may be a calumny, but it was commonly said that they were originally slated for steerage.

In the bow of the boat, where even steerage quarters leave off, there was some vacant space beneath the booms and winches on the deck above. This had been designated as nothing less than "third-class smoking room." There carpenters hastily constructed rude stalls for poor steeds like me. But the officials called them berths, those hundred double-decker, coffin-like affairs with thin, straw-stuffed mattresses. If any uneasy sleeper had ever swung a strong arm, he would have knocked out half a dozen of his fellows with one fell blow, so close to one another were those narrow bunks.

There was not so much as a nail on which to hang our clothes. Laundry was done only twice on the trip. Personal cleanliness was a problem because of lack of water, which was turned on in the washrooms for only one hour in the morning and a half hour in the evening. Men stood in long queues, hoping to be able to wash face and hands before the deadline. Only by carrying a bottle of water away to some less-congested corner, could one manage to shave. The bath was open once in ten days.

After days in the steaming tropics, the ship reeked with foul air below decks. Passengers slept on the hatches, on the decks, in chairs, everywhere but in the quarters assigned to them. True, the *Asama Maru* was not built to accommodate such a multitude. For that very reason, the Japanese Government should have agreed to the American Government's proposal to charter a larger, neutral vessel. But even a neutral ship may spy? Every man for his own specialty: Japan should know!

Our first stopping place was Hong Kong. How good the sight of our vessel must have been to the Americans waiting there on the roofs of houses, all watching our unhurried progress! At last we stood off Stanley Point, opposite the Center House of the Maryknoll Fathers. It was then in the hands of the Japanese Army. A lighter put out from shore, and a committee came aboard to arrange the details of the transfer.

During the afternoon, ferryboats scurried back and forth, bringing out the Hong Kong contingent. We had only to look at the distraught and haggard faces of the newcomers, to know the nature of their internment. A few Maryknoll missioners who could not return to their missions in the interior, or who were already en route to the United States when war broke out, came aboard, with some of the Maryknoll Sisters who had been stationed in Hong Kong. We spent the night anchored off Stanley Point. Next morning the *Asama Maru* breasted the waves, her compass set for French Indo-China.

On the third of July, we arrived at Saigon. The variety of harbor craft flying the Rising Sun, and the scarcity of Frenchmen in responsible positions, eloquently betrayed the abject status of that nominally French colonial possession. Native boats, full of tropical fruits, converged on our vessel, and we had a pleasant time bargaining over the side with the vendors, and pulling up our luscious purchases in buckets and bamboo baskets. In the afternoon, a ship bearing the evacuees from Thailand steamed up the river, and within a few hours the transfer of the *Asama Maru's* last lot of passengers was smoothly effected. We left port in the forenoon of an inglorious Fourth of July. Only a few missionary patriots in steerage class ventured to sing "The Star-Spangled Banner"—a rash demonstration, at which the diplomats were horrified.

At dawn on July 9, our ship entered the heavily mined waters off Singapore. A corvette guided us through the narrow channel, while another covered our tracks. The *Asama Maru* dropped anchor, ninety miles from the city. The Italian vessel, *Conte Verde*, carrying the evacuees from Shanghai and the hinterlands of China, rode at anchor near by. The Italian and Japanese captains, as well as the Swiss delegates, exchanged courtesy calls.

Two children, a little Dutch boy and girl whose parents were thought to be aboard the *Asama Maru*, came over on the launch, only to be turned away. After their long, bewildering trip from Shanghai, they were interned in Singapore to await the arrival of the British exchange ship. Fifty Americans—yes a hundred of them —gladly would have assumed responsibility for these tiny globetrotters. But in time of war even charity is circumscribed. Two days later, having taken on water and supplies, we left for Portuguese East Africa, far across the Indian Ocean.

Heading toward the Sunda Straits, we passed close to a sunken vessel; only the top of its mast was visible. We were sailing dangerous waters, which had witnessed the fury of the battle of the Java Sea. The Indian Ocean was rough with mountainous rollers, and not a few of the passengers were seasick for days. Our morale was at a low ebb during those two trying weeks. As we neared Madagascar, our spirits rose. Land again! But should we be allowed to disembark?

On July 25, a month to the day after our departure from Yokohama, we sighted the verdant shores of Mozambique. The harbor of Lourenco Marques, the capital, was alive with shipping. As the *Asama Maru* entered the harbor with land-hungry hundreds lining the ship's rails, the crew of the American tanker *Malaya* cheered, and the whistles of that battle-scarred ranger of the deep screeched welcome again and again. Old Glory was flying in the breeze, and the crowded decks of the Japanese vessel acclaimed with unrestrained cheers that beautiful symbol of our native land. Other United States and British vessels in the harbor joined in the demonstration, and the waters of that far African port rang with the cries of freedom.

Lourenco Marques is a tidy little seaport town, in the southeastern corner of Portuguese East Africa. There the exchange of evacuees from the United States and Japan took place. There the three thousand passengers of the three ships passed in review, before unbiased neutrals. Those who saw the Americans arrive were able to compare their condition with that of the Japanese, and to compare the amount of the baggage they carried with the amount of luggage allowed to the Japanese. The obvious facts told which nationals had been maltreated.

Frank Gervasi, an American correspondent in that far-off corner of the world, is said to have expressed the general opinion in bluntly honest words: "They (the Japanese) looked like Fifth Avenue and the Loop, while our people looked like Bowery bums." And Mr. Gervasi did not know the half of it!

During the few days the exchange ships tarried at Lourenco Marques, the author had a last chore to do before breaking bonds with Japan. One of the Hong Kong evacuees, unable to forget the sights that he had witnessed during the siege of the British island, went straightway to a newspaper office with a story of Japanese atrocities. The clerk in the newspaper office was a woman who understood less English than she would admit. She wrote up the account in such a way as to implicate some of the author's fellow missioners in the release of the story to the press. Fearing that a garbled report would reach Japan and redound to the harm of American missioners and other innocent individuals still interned there, I felt it my duty to acquaint the Japanese Ambassador with the facts.

The former Japanese Ambassador to the United States —Admiral Nomura—was accompanying the Japanese nationals who were being repatriated. It was impossible to meet him in the town, for he was too well attended by solicitous aides. Besides, a spirit of hostility was mounting daily, while the two groups of evacuees waited in Lourenco Marques. Stories of the extreme ill-usage suffered by many American internees in Japan were circulating, and the Japanese repatriates, who had no cause for complaint about their own treatment in the United States, began shamefacedly to avoid all Americans. After much maneuvering, I got aboard the Japanese ship and requested an interview with Admiral Nomura. The Ambassador's secretary promised me five minutes for an interview, but the admiral himself was most cordial, and chatted with me and my companion for almost an hour. He noted in writing my explanation of the newspaper incident.

Then I went on to discuss the illegal actions of the Japanese police in Japan, against the Christian religion, particularly as those actions affected my parish in Shiga County. Admiral Nomura promised to refer the matter to the Tokyo Government. Several times he declared, "If any injustice has been done, I am sure it will be rectified."

While we talked, I gathered the impression that the former Ambassador was not certain about his own future in Japan. He admitted as much when, with the suggestion of a smile, he said, "I am not sure that I shall have any influence after I return to Japan; but if I have, I promise that justice will be done."

Admiral Nomura then referred to a matter that has since become known to the public through the memoirs of Cordell Hull, wartime Secretary of State in the Roosevelt Cabinet. The admiral remarked that Bishop James E. Walsh, of Maryknoll, and his vicar general, Father James M. Drought, had striven valiantly, although in an unofficial capacity, to halt the worsening of relations between the United States and Japan. "Convey my sincere gratitude to them," the admiral said, "for their unflagging efforts in behalf of peace."

Then this man, who only a few years earlier had been tested and proved in the thick of war, continued a little ruefully, it seemed to me: "Now the fighters must fight. But peace will come. It must come. And there are men in the Japanese Army and Navy who are desirous of peace—men who did not want this war."

As we rose to go, Admiral Nomura extended his hand. "Now we shake hands as human beings," he said. "The next time, let us hope, it will be as friends."

The Japanese ships were the first to leave. We departed two days later, bidding an affectionate farewell to Lourenco Marques, that kindly refuge of purple bougainvillaea and whitewashed garden walls. We sailed on the clean and hospitable exchange ship, the Swedish *Gripsholm*.

Aboard the *Gripsholm*, most of our men were in steerage class, four to six in a room. The missioners had proved that they could rough it. Although the air was very stuffy, and it was difficult to sleep in many of the steerage cabins, conditions were a hundred per cent better than the conditions on the *Asama Maru*. On the Swedish ship, we had running water all day long. The baths were always open, and the swimming pool was always available. The fare, too, was much superior to the table aboard the Japanese ship.

The next ten days passed rather uneventfully. Early on August 10, our ship glided into the beautiful harbor of Rio de Janeiro. Not far distant, on a mountain peak, stood the colossal figure of Christ, the Prince of Peace, with His arms outstretched in a protecting gesture over that great Brazilian metropolis. At Rio most of our South American friends disembarked. We had passed many happy and constructive hours with them. During two days in this port, we were greatly impressed by the discipline and progressive spirit of the Brazilian people; and they made no secret of the fact that they admire and like North Americans.

In the afternoon of August 11, the *Gripsholm* started on the last lap of our eighteen-thousand-mile trip. The next two weeks passed quickly and quietly. Once we went off course to investigate a burning hulk that might have been a freighter—or as some conjectured, a mothership for German submarines. There was no human being in sight, and the officers on the bridge could not distinguish any sign of life on the burning vessel, around which we circled many times. This incident impressed the war more sharply on our consciousness.

At dawn on August 25 (1942), seventy days after we had gone aboard at Yokohama, we saw, shimmering in the distance, the shoreline of the country of our desire. All passengers crowded the decks as the Statue of Liberty came into view. At the sight of that symbol of our native land, the hearts of all true Americans were thrilled to the core, and many eyes were moist with tears. And some of us remembered the poet's words:

> "Breathes there the man with soul so dead,
> Who never to himself hath said:
> 'This is my own, my native land'? "

Still, as we Catholic missioners crowded the hushed deck rails straining for a glimpse of home after an absence of ten years and more, we were torn between two conflicting desires. Deep down in our hearts there was a feeling of tumultuous exultation because we were home. Yet at the same time we experienced a sense of piercing loneliness, for we were exiled from the mission fields and the people of our predilection. True, we had suffered in the midst of our chosen people. But our sufferings were only a shadow of theirs. The militarists who persecuted their own people and us, we leave to the judgment of history.

As we stood there on the deck of the *Gripsholm,* looking out to the fair land of America where our ancestors had fought to win religious and democratic freedom, we felt that on some future day Japan, too, would emerge victorious from a similar struggle. Then, we thought, the sons of Yamato might pride themselves on being Christians, if not Christian democrats—a vocation to which they might have aspired during that breathless interlude from 1878 to 1888, if the Western nations had not sickened them with the stench of power politics.

12. "After Rain the Ground Gets Hard"

MUCH WATER has passed under the proverbial bridge since August of 1942. World War II is over. And now at long last, after these several years of tutelage, the hour of Christianity and Christian democracy has struck in Nippon. In the dazzling dawn of the cosmic age, the people of Japan had beheld a great vision. True, they had discovered in the clarity of that merciless light the stark ruin of their homeland. But at the same time they had descried, in the not-unforeseeable future, the emerging pattern of a New Japan. Like the phoenix arising from the ashes of its funeral pyre, Japan is destined to emerge from the abyss of her desolation to newness of life. Such is the firm conviction of an indomitable race.

After the initial shock of their discovery that our victorious soldiers, far from being fiends incarnate, were honorable men, a timid thrill of hope, soon lost in a wave of mounting enthusiasm, coursed through the ranks of the vanquished Japanese. In the glow of that enthusiasm, which gathers vitality and volume as months go by, the greatest progress in the rehabilitation and rejuvenation of Japan is possible. Fired by their new vision, the Japanese people are literally swept on from one success to another, in the transformation of their national life. To quote the wisdom of the ancients, "fire makes room for itself."

In this unparalleled process of national change, those who knew pre-war Japan are struck, first of all, by the complete revolution in Japanese thought. After the Russo-Japanese War, largely because of the unsatisfactory peace concluded at Portsmouth, the popularity of the United States began to wane. Then came the disastrous disillusionment of the Exclusion Acts—a terrible and needless hurt, from which the proud race of Nippon never recovered. The indignation of the Japanese people swelled tenfold when, after we had barred them from our own country, we insisted that they had no right to occupy Manchuria for purposes of immigration and colonization. When later the United States openly sided with China, even going so far as to arm that nation against Japan, their indignation knew no bounds. And when, finally, the United States proceeded to erect high tariff walls against Japanese goods, thus making it impossible for Japan's people to maintain their comparatively high standard of living, Japan could tolerate no more. The bombing of Pearl Harbor—for which we were not prepared because of our own criminal negligence—was, in the eyes of most Japanese people, merely a counterattack in a "war" already undertaken by the United States.

In the fever of the conflict, rumors of atrocities flew

thick and fast, leading the uninformed Japanese to regard Americans as barbarians. When, in the final stages of the war, all their great cities except one were crushed into rubble by the long series of bombardments from November, 1944, to August, 1945—when, on three occasions a total of more than 120,000 people were burned to death—they were unalterably convinced of our utter inhumanity. The culmination of their tragedy, on August 14, 1945, only served to confirm the Japanese in their erroneous conviction.

From seven o'clock in the morning, hour after hour on that fateful day, the ominous announcement came over the radio: "At noon listen to your radio. . . . All, without exception, listen! . . . His Majesty, the Son of Heaven, will speak! . . . A most important message from His Majesty. . . ."

Now it is noon! Solemn hour, indeed; perhaps the most solemn in the checkered course of Japan's long history. Amid the woes of war, a besieged nation pauses with one accord to hear the gracious words of imperial encouragement. "One more effort!" That is what the Japanese were sure His Majesty, the Emperor, would say.

A faint mechanical sound is audible at first, like the quiet whirr of a needle cutting a phonograph record. There is high drama here. Everyone is quick to sense it. But few in the listening multitude have any inkling of the nature of the drama behind this little act in a monumental tragedy. That phonograph disc had been cut with the greatest secrecy in the vast middle of the previous night.

The firebrands of the young officers' clique had learned that a recording was to be made, and they had resolved to destroy it. They would appeal!—from Emperor misinformed to Emperor informed. In the frenzy of their rage, those young men, who had never known the danger of actual battle or tasted the gall of defeat, invaded the premises of the imperial palace. They stirred up revolt among the soldiers of the palace guard, and slaughtered all who dared to stay the progress of their mad quest.

Meanwhile, hidden with a few of his trusted advisers, in a tiny tea house located in an isolated part of the moated palace grounds, was the man whom impartial history one day may deem the bravest of contemporary monarchs. Emperor Hirohito literally took his life in his hands, when he dared to record the proclamation of surrender.

Now, at high noon, the awesome voice of the Emperor breaks the silence—that high-pitched voice never heard before by those eighty million of his countrymen. They stand in reverential pose, hands by their sides, heads bowed. Tears are in the eyes of many, as these words fall on their ears: "It little matters what may befall my person. . . . I am no longer able to tolerate the sufferings of my people. . . . It is for this reason that I have accepted the conditions of the Potsdam Declaration . . ."

The thunderbolt of that imperial message shook Japan to its foundations. The war, then, was lost? Yes, lost—when all the while the people had been told that their country was winning it! Lost—through those long, hectic months of indescribable dread, when the B-29's ranged up and down their countryside, spreading death and devastation. They had been duped—duped by their own leaders! Terrible thought! And perhaps they had been deceived from the beginning?

A nation-wide quest for the truth began, and in all this inquiry there was not a little soul-searching. When the lurid tale of the atrocities perpetrated by their own army and navy personnel began to trickle back to Japan, the people murmured, "*Tembatsu*"—"The punishment of Heaven!"

A member of the imperial family summed up the amazing change in the national psychology in these words, "If we had been victorious, it would have been disastrous for ourselves and for the world at large!"

Such a statement required clear-sighted courage.

At the risk of belaboring the point, the author has thought it well to emphasize this complete transformation in the psychology of the Japanese people. It is something the like of which history has not witnessed before; and the like of which we probably shall never see again, until the emancipation of the people of Russia.

Only in the light of this monumental change in Japanese thought—this national conviction that the people had been shamelessly betrayed, and that a lifetime is too short a while in which to ferret out the facts—can we understand the consuming hunger for new ideas, on the part of the people of Japan. They have the rare, national ability spontaneously to seek new goals, when old objectives have failed them. It is this ability that is making Japan's conversion to Christianity and Christian democracy appear so natural.

In all this striving toward new goals, which at first will be indistinct and difficult of attainment, there is bound to be not a little confusion. In an interview with Roger N. Baldwin, published in *The Reader's Digest*, Yukio Ozaki, one of Japan's elder liberal statesmen, has drawn an amusing picture of the present scene: "What a mixture is Japan—old and new, feudal and modern, ox-carts and limousines, busses and rickshas, kimonos and bobby-sox. Inside our heads it is just like that, too. It will take a long time to get us all going in the same direction."

In spite of this confusion, Japan's direction has been set very definitely. In rationalizing her defeat, Japan has found it necessary to attribute our superiority to the very thing of which she thought she had a monopoly—spiritual strength. Thus her steps are orientated toward all that is best in our democratic tradition. And since she rightly feels that our democracy is bound up with our Christianity, Japan is disposed anew to hear more about the Christian religion.

This remarkable spirit of inquiry is focused upon the field of religious and philosophical speculation. This new interest, on the part of men in general and the intelligentsia in particular, opens up a new vista to the spread of Christianity. For a long time, the men of Japan had manifested meager interest in the Christian religion. In pre-war years the congregations of Christian churches were largely composed of the devout sex, in about the same proportion as that in the first Christian congregation at the foot of the cross—three women to one man. In the new Japan, however, men are no longer ashamed to reveal their interest in religion. This is especially true of the educated class. Articles on the Christian religion appear regularly in current intellectual magazines, such as *Shinro*, and *Tembo*, and these articles are devoured by the intelligentsia.

In October of 1945, Professor Tokuryu Yamanouchi, Dean of Philosophy at the Imperial University of Kyoto, approached the Reverend Vincent Pouliot, O.P., a Catholic priest who had matriculated as a research student at the University in 1941, asking him to volunteer his services in acquainting the student body with the principles of Thomistic philosophy. A Chair of Catholic Philosophy seemed to be the answer to this need.

An "angel" appeared in the person of a devout Buddhist, Mr. Shikaji Hiraki. This Japanese gentleman realized that the best contribution he could make to the spiritual rejuvenation of his country would be to afford the youth of Japan the opportunity to study a genuine philosophy. So enthusiastic was the response, that Father Pouliot has been obliged to organize a *schola* at St. Thomas House of Studies, for students who were unable to attend his lectures at the university. The interest of his students in the philosophy of Saint Thomas Aquinas may be gauged from the fact that many of them follow both courses.

There is, however, in this discussion of the Christian religion on the philosophical level, a danger to which we should not close our eyes. In Japan as elsewhere, religion is a subject on which every half-baked individual who styles himself a philosopher is prone to pontificate. So it is with Christianity in Nippon. Left-wing materialists are quick to pass unfavorable judgment on the conclusions of Christian philosophy, thus reviving the old prejudices under the disguise of the new learning. On the other hand, there are the sympathetic but too-superficial writers who, by their irresponsibility and shallowness, play into the hands of the critics. In all this philosophical speculation, Catholics especially must be diligent in setting the proper tone and giving the necessary guidance. Otherwise, the whole process will degenerate into arid, wordy nonsense, completely dissipating the deep concern with religion—a concern now shared by many of the youth of New Japan.

The persistent partisan spirit that still animates the body of Japanese educators is clearly seen in the scholastic program voted by the Diet, early in 1948. This program has introduced a course in "sociology," the scope of which is to teach the social aspect of religion. The emphasis, however, is on Buddhism and Shinto, which are presented as "national religions"; whereas, Christianity is described as a "foreign religion"! Furthermore, the program prescribes the singing of Buddhist and Shintoist hymns on holidays, and provides for pilgrimages to the religious centers of Japan. When we consider the fundamentally Shintoistic subject matter of this government-inspired course in "sociology," and advert to the fact that its implementation will be left entirely to teachers who may be ignorant of Christianity, even if not disposed to disregard or despise it, we have reason to suspect the motives of the Japanese Ministry of Education. Catholic leaders in Japan have stigmatized the whole new curriculum, of which this program is a part, as a flagrant violation of the Japanese Constitution, which prohibits the state from engaging in religious education (Chapter 3, Article XVIII).

Further proof of this partisan spirit can be found in two new history texts. Early in 1948, the Ministry of Education made those texts mandatory in all public and private schools.

The first of these books is entitled *Kuni No Ayumi—Progress of the Country*. It is openly hostile to Christianity. It makes the following very serious misrepresentations:

1. Christianity is incompatible with Japanese traditions.

2. The anti-Christian persecutions were necessary, because the Christian daimios constituted a threat to the security of the country.

3. The revolt of the persecuted Christians of Shimabara was an uprising against the established authority.

The second text is entitled *Seiyo No Rekishi—History of the West*. It is eloquent of evolutionary and progressivist bias. According to Father William A. Kaschmitter, M.M., representative of the National Catholic Welfare Conference News Service in Japan, the following pseudoscientific assumptions are propounded as factual truths:

1. Man is totally simian in his origin.

2. "We modern men can no longer believe in the stories of the Gospels, such as the birth of Christ, His miracles and His resurrection."

3. The persecutions of ancient Rome (the book devotes only five pages to Roman history) were justified, because of the waywardness of the first Christians.

4. The rise of Christianity must be attributed to political alliances of Popes and monarchs.

5. The birth of civilization followed the "darkness of the Middle Ages."

6. The humanists freed men from the yoke of the priests, who prevented them from acquiring scientific knowledge.

Such is the outmoded trash that is now finding its way into the hands of the children and youth of Japan. The fact that such unscientific and anti-Christian literature can be published under the very noses of the Occupation authorities makes one wonder who is taking care of the watchman's job when the watchman isn't taking care. This is not intended as an invidious criticism; incidents of the kind are bound to happen under any wartime regime. Already some corrective action has been taken in regard to these *Social Study Guide Books*. But the publication of such texts serves to point up the contention that, beneath the surface of all the optimistic educational reforms now afoot in Japan, there runs a deep crosscurrent of reaction.

True, the war has freed the Christian schools from many former restrictions. Now a Christian institution of learning may house a chapel. Religion may be taught in the classrooms. And the students are no longer under compulsion to attend superstitious or quasi-religious functions in the national shrines. But a great deal of the old scholastic legislation must be erased from the law books, before Christians will be able to enjoy the full-blown fruits of religious emancipation.

In pre-war Japan, the Christian religion could exercise only the slightest influence upon the children of elementary-school age. Primary schools conducted under Church auspices were not tolerated, except where they were associated with already established secondary schools. The latter were not numerous, inasmuch as they were denied access to public funds and were required to deposit considerable sums of money before they might open their doors. In spite of heavy expenses, there are at present fifty-nine Catholic secondary and vocational schools in Japan; fifteen of them are for boys, and forty-four are for girls. Although these schools exert a profound influence, they reach only four thousand boys and twelve thousand girls out of 3,500,000 children in attendance at secondary schools. Not all Catholic secondary schools are able to provide primary departments; consequently, the picture of primary education is even more depressing than that of secondary education.

Primary education in Japan is still practically a state monopoly. The first and only independent grammar school under Catholic auspices was opened as late as 1947, on the little island of Madara, the population of which is almost entirely Catholic. This departure from established policy was permitted because the local public school had been destroyed during the war. Thus, the number of children who come under the influence of the Catholic Church during their primary-school years is comparatively insignificant. Of more than twelve million attending primary schools, less than twenty-five hundred children are enrolled in Catholic institutions.

Approximately seven thousand younger children are in attendance at one hundred Catholic kindergartens, and as many more are enrolled in Sunday Schools; but the children of Japan, by and large, are still untouched by Catholic influence. Protestant institutions of learning, while they possess higher enrollments in the secondary and advanced departments, likewise fail to exert a proportionate influence over children in the primary grades. In short, Christianity has not been able, and still is unable, to reach a vast majority of the thirty-seven per cent of the Japanese population who are under fourteen years of age. Surely, this situation poses a problem that is bound to affect profoundly the Christian and democratic future of New Japan.

The greatest diffusion of secular knowledge will not be enough. No less a personage than Doctor Kotaro Tanaka, one of Japan's legal lights and a former Minister of Education, frankly admits the supreme need of religious education in post-war Nippon. In a vigorous indictment of the evils in Japanese society (which appeared in the *Asahi Hyoron* for December, 1947), the learned gentleman stated that secular education is powerless to cope with this inheritance received from the old regime.

"Science alone," observed Doctor Tanaka, "is not the panacea to cure these evils, as many Japanese commonly believe. Science furnishes techniques and conveniences; but whether or not it contributes to the welfare of society, depends on the purposes for which it is used. These purposes have to be set from lofty and universally valid points of view; they have to be subject to objective norms. The Japanese have learned scientific methods and know how to handle machines. But all their acquired technology has not made the people happier; on the contrary, it was mainly responsible for the last war.

"What the Japanese have not learned is the ultimate purpose of life. Our university education has been characterized by excessive specialization, while our high schools have been used to drill automata. . . . Our natural scientists, with few exceptions, have been simple-minded materialists, and our sociologists have been materialistic and pragmatistic in their entire method. . . . In the field of economics, most Japanese scholars belong to the school of historical materialism; and no other school, it appears, is allowed to exist.

"Only wisdom creates and unites men, and it emanates from the contemplation of, and reflection on, the final cause through metaphysics and religion." (Quoted from the *Missionary Bulletin,* March, 1948)

Doctor Tanaka certainly has diagnosed not only the illness of his own race, but a Western malady as well. Many even in our own land have lost sight of the "final cause" of our existence. Until men everywhere regain that vision, which everyone had in the so-called Dark

13. "Fire Makes Room for Itself"

THE MAJOR BURDEN of Christianity's program in Japan, insofar as it must be implemented by the resources and personnel of foreign mission societies, would appear to have fallen to the lot of the Catholic Church, which now enjoys an unprecedented opportunity for service. While Protestant missionaries are slow to return to their posts, because economic conditions make family life difficult if not impossible, Catholic missioners are seizing time by the forelock. According to a report issued by the Catholic Rehabilitation Committee in January, 1948, a total of 326 Catholic missioners had been cleared for Japan by the Occupation authorities. Most of these priests, Brothers, and Sisters were already on the field; and there is the promise of more recruits to follow them in the not-distant future.

Japanese Catholics are enthusiastically looking for the return of the foreign missioners who before the war labored so zealously in their midst. The Japanese clergy, too, are frankly anxious to welcome additional foreign personnel. All find in their associations with the foreign missioners a stimulating experience. Side by side, Catholics, both Japanese and foreign, labor for the rehabilitation of the Church in every part of Japan.

On the other hand, Japanese Protestants appear not

to be of one mind in regard to the return of foreign missionaries. Thus, the Reverend Akaiwa Sakae, writing in the monthly review, *Choryu,* for December of last year, says that, for the future of the Christian religion, he hopes that "foreign missions will refrain from aiding the growth of Christianity in Japan, if they really wish it to develop soundly. . . . Pecuniary aid and professional ministers of the foreign-mission boards are only harmful to a healthy growth. They weaken our determination and enervate our faith."

Nowhere in Japan was the return of Catholic missioners welcomed with more genuine enthusiasm than in the Ryukyu (Loochoo) Islands, where the American Capuchins of the Detroit Province are laboring. During the thirteen years that followed the forcible expulsion of Canadian Franciscans by the Japanese military—who wished to construct fortifications in spite of treaty prohibitions—there had been no Mass on Oshima, the strategic island nearest to Japan proper. It was December, 12, 1934, when the sons of Saint Francis celebrated their last Mass in the beautiful brick church of Naze, which represented a labor of twenty years. Literally hounded out of the islands, after their rectories had been set afire several times, and local merchants had been forbidden to sell them food, the Canadian missioners left Oshima. After their departure, the Catholic population of the North Loochoos lived through years of loneliness and positive persecution.

But eventually the missioners returned, as they always do. On Christmas Eve of 1947, the American Capuchins were about to celebrate Midnight Mass in Naze. Then in walked an old Japanese woman, who had a most interesting tale to tell. Ten years earlier, she had carried off the altar linens and the sacred vessels, lest they be profaned by sacrilegious hands. No amount of official questioning, threatening, and ransacking of her humble lodging could discover her secret keep. But now a better day was about to dawn. And this Oriental daughter of St. Nicholaus returned to the church of Naze, trundling her bundle of treasure-trove to rejoice the hearts of all the faithful Christians. So it was that Christmas came again to Oshima, in the Ryukyus.

Other candles of cheer have been lit, all the way from the far southern isles to the northernmost province of Japan. And in the widening glow of those candles, we can descry our brethren in the Faith, toiling and moiling in little towns and great, amid the aftermath of war, for the rehabilitation of their little corner of Christ's kingdom here on earth.

Thus on Kyushu—southernmost island of the four that comprise the area of Japan proper—in the "holy land" of Nagasaki, we behold Catholics laboring with their own hands to rebuild their ruined churches. At the foot of Mount Tate, sacred to the memory of the six-and-twenty crosses raised against a feudal sky, lies a mound of rubble that was once the great church of the Immaculate Conception of the Blessed Virgin Mary. In 1934, the author baptized six infants in that hallowed shrine. He cannot help wondering where those little ones are now. Are they, too, wrestling with the rubble in that glorious effort to rebuild the church around which their young lives used to revolve?

On Honshu, the main island, in its city of Yamaguchi, where Saint Francis Xavier centuries ago lit the first taper of Christian truth, new faith is found. Apparently the great apostle worked through a wartime incident concerning his statue. During the recent conflict, Japan was so hard pressed for materials wherewith to maintain her war machine, that junkyards disappeared rapidly. Then everything the militarists could lay their hands on became legitimate loot. In Yamaguchi they stopped short of melting the bronze statue erected to the memory of Francis Xavier, but they did not hesitate to strip the monument of its metal medallions. According to an eye-witness, tragedy and irony marked the spoliation of Xavier's shrine.

"The monument offered a sad spectacle," observes the witness. "In the center of it, there had been placed a Shinto altar, with the classic Japanese adornment of fruits and cereals. Before the altar a Shinto priest intoned a prayer for the purpose of placating the spirit of Xavier. Representatives of the Provincial Office and other civil authorities stood behind the priest. At the termination of the prayer, the mayor publicly invoked the saint for pardon, saying that he no doubt would understand and pity the necessity that impelled Japan to remove the metal from his monument for the purpose of accomplishing the ideals of a universal peace."

Now the whole city is desirous of making amends by restoring the statue of the saint. No group of missioners could do as much as the restoration campaign is doing, to focus the attention of this Oriental metropolis on the Christian religion. So the great apostle who twice was deified by the pagan priests of Yamaguchi— long ago by the Buddhists, and in our time by the Shintoists—still labors among the people who were his "delight." We can not help feeling that his modern ministry in Yamaguchi will bear great fruit, because Xavier never was known to surrender, except when in the course of his apostolic *jiujitsu* he retreated only in order to stage an irresistible come-back.

To the northeast on the same island, is the wilderness of Hiroshima. There, too, where mankind first beheld the awful glory of the cosmic dawn, candles of faith are lit again. One might think that in Hiroshima, at least, the Japanese could not be blamed for hating the religion allegedly professed by the nation that loosed the atomic bomb. Yet—according to the report of the Jesuit Fathers to whom this mission is entrusted—instead of hating Christianity, the survivors of Hiroshima have an even greater interest in it. They are realistic enough to know that we dropped the atomic bomb not because we are Christians, but in spite of the fact that we claim fellowship with Christ. Just as many of their ancestors saw, beyond the buccaneers of Portugal and Spain, the genuine followers of Christ, so must they see beyond the lunatic fringe of intransigent capitalists, chaotic communists, unprincipled politicians, and professional bureaucrats, the great, good people of America, who bear no lasting grudge against any child of God. *Christus vincit*—"Christ conquers"—in His own inscrutable way.

In the mission field of Hiroshima is the city of Okayama, on the Inland Sea. There the American Sisters of Notre Dame of the Waltham, Massachusetts, province, are again conducting their excellent school for young ladies. All these brave women were at their posts when war broke out, and they were interned almost two years before being repatriated. The author remembers one of them telling how, in the internment camp, she used to close her eyes at meal time, when boiled frog was served, and, with the greatest attempt at self-deception, say, "This is delicious roast chicken!"

With the new equality that has come to the women of Japan, is the right to examine the credentials of the Christian religion. In pre-war years, no young lady of marriageable age could dream of receiving Baptism without the consent of her parents. They, if they consented at all, were prone to condition their permission on the consent of their daughter's future husband;

and there was no reason to expect "honorable master's" consent, unless he were docile to the inspirations of the Holy Ghost. But now the women of Japan are free at least to investigate the Christian religion. In view of their natural attraction for what is noble and high-minded, we can look forward to many conversions to the Catholic Faith in such excellent schools as Sacred Heart Girls' Academy in Okayama.

Farther east, in the Himeji sector south of Kobe, where the American Baptist missionaries were early at work, an influx of missioners from Belgium is raising the standard of the cross anew. The Immaculate Heart Missioners were assigned to this field last year because it was impossible for them to continue their work in North China and Mongolia, where a mad, murderous campaign is in progress under the expert direction of the Communists—those "good" people who the world over are slaughtering the proletariat because they love them so. Not for nothing have the Immaculate Heart Missioners been tried in the fiery furnace of persecution in Russian Mongolia and Japanese Jehol. The Mongolian brutalization of their converts in a land practically closed even to Chinese for the past twenty years; the Japanese exploitation of their parishioners in the poppy fields of Jehol; the desultory murders of their fellow missioners by Communists in the fastnesses of Manchuria —all these hardships have tried and tested and readied the men of Belgium for their new apostolate in Nippon.

Across the straits, to the southwest of Himeji, lies the island of Shikoku. In this territory, which long has been a stronghold of Buddhism, the devoted Spanish Dominicans labored with the most meager results. But now Shikoku is looking up, like the rest of Japan. People there are interested in Christianity, and the missioners feel that they will make excellent converts, judging by their previous steadfastness in the Buddhist religion. To help them reap this ripening harvest, the veteran Spanish missioners joyfully look forward to the coming of the American Oblates of Mary Immaculate and the Franciscan Friars of the Atonement.

Now we are seeking candles of faith among the rubble heaps of ruined Kobe and half-gutted Osaka, the second city in Japan. In this territory, long the preserve of the Paris Foreign Missions Society, the development of the Catholic Church has been so thorough that the local native clergy will soon be numerous enough to care for the cities of Osaka and Kobe. In other sections of this large diocese, however, the services of foreign missioners are still needed, and the arrival of the Immaculate Heart Fathers in the Himeji district is a timely contribution to this need.

Among congregations of women, the Franciscan Missionaries of Mary, in particular, are extending their work in the diocese of Osaka. In the autumn of 1946, they opened a school of practical and fine arts for girls in the city of Kobe; and in the following spring, they adopted Star of the Sea School, which had been under the direction of the Sisters of the Infant Jesus. The latter excellent community, which lost twenty-one Sisters in the atomic bombing of Nagasaki, was obliged to give up the school because of lack of personnel. In June of the same year (1947), the Franciscan Missionaries of Mary (who in October, 1948, celebrated the fiftieth anniversary of their arrival in Japan) undertook the direction of the International Hospital in Kobe.

In near-by Osaka, the Pittsburgh of Japan, one thinks of molten steel and giant blast furnaces. In that war-girt metropolis of blazing crucibles, the gold in an old man's soul was sorely tried—and not found wanting. For Osaka was witness to the martyrdom of *Père* Bousquet, a member of the Paris Foreign Missions Society.

The author does not hesitate to describe the death of this venerable French priest as martyrdom, because such is the conviction entertained by many Japanese. It is common knowledge that Father Bousquet was seized by the jingo police of Osaka for the crime of insisting that God is superior to the sun goddess *(Amaterasu-omi-kami)*, the chief deity of Shinto. And it is widely assumed that this aged champion of the one, true God died under torture, because the secret police were quite adept at releasing prisoners in danger of death, lest their demise behind the bars excite the suspicions of the public. Monsignor Tatewaki Toda, the Vicar Apostolic of Sapporo, and Reverend Rinzo Onomura, a Protestant clergyman likewise stationed in Sapporo, were imprisoned on a similar charge, but the palm of martyrdom was not reserved for these brave men.

Twenty miles due east from Osaka is Nara, the first capital of Japan. In that stronghold of the old religions, Christianity made little headway. There the Catholic Church was known more for its Oriental architecture than for anything else. But the new interest in religion has insinuated itself into the ancient place of Buddhist pilgrimage and now, where formerly two or three converts were the yearly harvest, a hundred candidates study the Catholic religion. So pronounced is the transformation in the people's psychology, that Father Sugihara, the Japanese pastor, has been invited to address conventions of Buddhist believers, on the subject of Christianity. The district of Nara is part of the mission entrusted to Maryknoll, the Catholic Foreign Mission Society of America.

Slightly northeast of Osaka, distant only an hour by train, is the metropolis of Kyoto, once the Western Capital, and still the cultural center of Japan. In this templed town, sacred to the mikados of old, the American missioners of Maryknoll are hard at work, eager to be in the fray after ten long years of marking time. In the words of Father Harold Felsecker, of Milwaukee, a pioneer in this territory, "A people deprived of material possessions must seek consolation in the things of the spirit." This quest for satisfaction in the spiritual comes naturally to the people of Kyoto, who are among the most cultured in Japan.

The cathedral church of St. Francis Xavier, located in the heart of Kyoto, is presently in charge of a Japanese Prefect Apostolic, Monsignor Paul Furuya, whose aged parents died so nobly in the bombing of Kobe. He is assisted by two Maryknoll priests—Reverend Michael J. McKillop, of Brooklyn, New York, and Reverend Leo J. Steinbach, of Chariton, Iowa—and a Maryknoll auxiliary, Brother Clement Hansan, of St. Mary's, Kansas. Before the war, these four would have sufficed to care for all the converts in the city of Kyoto; but now they are hard pressed to supervise the post-war activities of their own parish alone, even with the assistance of a Japanese Sister and three lay catechists. Now a new day has dawned.

During the entire course of the war, only two hundred people found their way to the Catholic Church in Kyoto; but now many more "students of the way" are embracing the Faith. Approximately three hundred adults are studying the catechism, while three hundred children are attending instructions on Saturday afternoons. The sight of the old edifice on Dry River-bed Road, crowded with people for each of the Sunday Masses, would gladden the heart of the veteran French missioner who, disheartened at the paucity of his congregation, made history by this soulful remark to a handful of the female faithful: "My dear widows, I

commiserate you on the death of your devoted husbands."

If there is any passage in the Gospel that applies to
Japan in general, and to Kyoto in particular, it is this
one: "The poor you have always with you." In Kyoto,
a city of two million inhabitants, the Maryknoll missioners have been trying to offer a modicum of relief to
people who have been subsisting on a minimum diet for
years. In the vanguard of this relief work, is Father Leo
Steinbach, the self-sacrificing organizer of the local St.
Vincent de Paul Society.

Early in February, 1947, Father Steinbach and his
zealous, native "twelve apostles" decided to tackle the
situation in a forthright manner that would be in keeping with the best traditions of apostolic folly. So they
went out into the countryside with nary scrip or staff,
bargaining with incredulous farmers. To these, the missioner and his helpers could offer only I.O.U.'s in pay-
ment for foodstuffs with which to feed the poor of the
less-favored metropolis. On the following Sunday, these
dauntless Vincentians appealed to the Catholics of the
cathedral parish, for alms to pay for the "borrowed
vegetables." Their hearts were gladdened by the generous response—5,000 yen.

The distribution of the food made a touching spectacle. Maryknoll's Father John C. Murrett, an eyewit-
ness, has described the scene for us.

"Mothers with little ones clinging to their sleeves, and

tears streaming down their cheeks, thanked our twelve apostles. Young husbands, earning scarcely enough to keep a household together, were mute in their gratitude. A pagan schoolteacher had come to see the vision, in which he could not believe at second hand. Now he asks if he may bring twelve poor families whose children he teaches at school—one family for each of the apostles. A native policeman elbowed his way forward, curiously observed the proceedings, then promised volubly that he would crack down on dark transactions—the Japanese equivalent of the American black market—and will divert the goods of the guilty to the Society of St. Vincent de Paul.

"In order to relieve the sting of poverty, the Vincentians are not above hinting that contributions to their work are gladly received. No one knows whether those who approach the contribution box put in or take out, but truth to tell the box is never empty. Like the flour bin of the saintly Cure of Ars, Father Steinbach's collection box always contains something on which to draw in time of need."

Thus it is, as Jesus said: "The poor you have always with you." "They will not always be poor," Father Murrett concludes, "but it certainly appears that we always shall have them with us."

West and north of the palace to which Saint Francis Xavier came on bleeding feet, are two more parishes without permanent church buildings or a sufficiency of priests. In the north of Kyoto, the parish of Takano is cared for by Reverend John C. Murrett, of Buffalo, New York. This parish is fast becoming a center for the university students, in whom the missioners find so much promise for the future of Japan. This was the only church in Kyoto that was not deprived of its pastor during the war, for the Reverend Patrick J. Byrne, M.M., never was obliged to leave his home. He was kept in domiciliary internment, and was not able to do justice to his charge during the war years. But when the Emperor had decreed surrender, Father Byrne in a timely radio broadcast was able to render signal service by conditioning the Japanese people for the arrival of the American Occupation forces.

The then Spiritual Father of Takano is now a Monsignor for the second time, and is Apostolic Visitor to Korea. There many hope he will succeed in helping to condition the Land of Morning Calm, at least south of the iron curtain on the thirty-eighth parallel, for the blessings of Christianity and Christian democracy.

East of Kyoto, across the mountains, lies the civil prefecture of Shiga, the author's old mission ground. In Otsu, the prefectural capital, the church of St. Mary of the Lake still queens it over the green slope above the blue sheen of Biwa. During the war the local police walled off the sanctuary, converting the church proper into an annex of the central police station. To the little congregation of Catholics, that spelled the end of the world; but in the designs of Providence, the taking over of St. Mary's Church by the Otsu police guaranteed its safety. The present incumbent of St. Mary's is Reverend John J. Walsh, of New Haven, Connecticut. This Maryknoller states that the little group of Catholic confessors who proved stanch during the trying pre-war years, have come into good repute now. According to Father Walsh, where once the faithful Catholics were strictly shunned, now fifty catechumens come to learn about the Faith.

On the same side of Lake Biwa, in Karasaki (Cape of Cathay), is situated the Maryknoll House of Study, which is directed by Reverend William F. Murphy, of Syracuse, New York. In this fisherman's paradise are stationed Father Joseph A. Hunt, of Brookline, Massachusetts; Father Clement P. Boesflug, of Bismarck, North Dakota; Father William M. Mackesy, of Lynn, Massachusetts; and the architect of the mission, Brother William Neary, of Pittsfield, Massachusetts. Father Hunt is a kind of perpetually bubbling missionary fountain. Wherever he goes through the mountain village of Shiga, the conversation is bound to turn to the Christian religion. So great is the interest stirred up by this peripatetic Padre that not a few Japanese of the region are gravitating to the Maryknoll House of Study, requesting instruction in the Faith.

On the other side of the lake, in the village of Kusatsu, the Japanese Sisters of the Visitation conduct a tuberculosis sanatorium. The dread disease, the scourge of pre-war Japan, claims so many victims everywhere that, long before this Maryknoll sanatorium had been completed, the management of a factory in the near-by town of Ishiyama requested that the accommodations be reserved for the factory's sick personnel. On the northern shore of the lake, in the city of Hikone, another man of Maryknoll is fishing for souls. Father Clarence J. Witte, of Richmond, Indiana, says that now the fishing is good, where in former days the nibbles were few and far between.

It is in neighboring Mie Prefecture, however, that the most spectacular developments in the Maryknoll Mission have taken place. On the day of his arrival, Father Thomas A. Barry, of Roxbury, Massachusetts, received an enthusiastic welcome from the people and officials of the provincial capital. The whole city of Tsu eagerly co-operated in the reconstruction of the mission buildings, which had been bombed out during the war. At the dedication of Father Barry's rectory-chapel, in addition to his confrere, Father Edmond L. Ryan, of Dorchester, Massachusetts, there were present the governor of the prefecture, the mayors of the six surrounding cities, local school principals, newspaper reporters, and leading business men. The city officials later financed the erection of an Old Folks' Home on property donated to the mission by the government. Surely, a great change has come over this inland city, where before the war only the military police paid any attention to Catholic missioners.

The next of Japan's great cities is Nagoya. There, as well as in the city of Niigata, on the Sea of Japan, the missioners of the Society of the Divine Word are zealously at work. In Niigata especially, the missioners have done much to foster the Catholic Boy Scout movement. In Tokyo, Father Karl Reitz, S.V.D., was happy to present the first Catholic Scouts of post-war Japan to the late Father Flanagan of Boys Town.

The diocese of Kanagawa, the cathedral city of which is ruined Yokohama, is entrusted to the Paris Foreign Missions Society. During the war the work in Yokohama received a serious setback, but the Brothers of Mary and the Sisters of St. Maur, in particular, are making heroic efforts to restore their excellent institutions of learning to pre-war levels of efficiency. In most of the outlying cities and towns, the various missionary enterprises are still functioning under the direction of veteran French missioners, who have spent thirty to forty years in Japan.

It is in near-by Tokyo, the nation's capital, that the strong pulse of Catholicism's second spring is most clearly felt. In Tokyo there is no department of missionary activity that has not received a definite stimulus. New churches, schools, dispensaries, orphanages, and a variety of establishments difficult to classify, are so many fruits of this most optimistic apostolate in Japan.

In the field of Catholic education, Sophia University, which is under the direction of the German Jesuits, is in the forefront of the Church's endeavor to give the Gospel to the intelligentsia of Nippon. Professors of this university occupy the Chair of Catholic Sciences recently established at the Imperial University of Tokyo.

Sophia University is operating again at full capacity, with eight hundred students enrolled. It provides courses in philosophy, literature, history, political economy, administrative sciences, and theology. Extension courses are given in journalism, as well as in social and economic science. Moreover, this Catholic institution offers a public course in sociology for the purpose of studying the Japanese labor question, with a view to applying the social principles enunciated in the Papal encyclicals. Furthermore, the university has established a settlement in the less-privileged ward of Mikawashima, where Italian Salesians have done good work during almost a score of years. In this quarter of the capital, the students work for the alleviation of the wretched conditions that long have existed there.

14. The Strong Arm of Charity

PRACTICAL CHARITY and social justice are the most pressing needs of the hour in post-war Japan—as everywhere else on earth. The Catholic Church in Japan is leaving no stone unturned in order to effect the realization of these two great Christian ideals. A joint pastoral issued on August 22, 1947, by the Japanese Bishops, brought these religious opportunities and needs into sharp focus.

"It is essential," declared the pastoral, "to work towards the realization of genuine social justice. Our first duty is to co-operate with the government in crushing the ruinous black market. . . . Hard work is the only way of meeting the difficulties. . . . Even among the faithful, the courageous and far-sighted social principles enunciated by the Popes are still widely unknown. . . . The root cause of our present calamity is the lack of charity."

One of the positive first fruits of the pastoral was an upsurge of interest in the work of the St. Vincent de Paul Society. While local chapters of this society have been at work in a number of missions, there has been no affiliation with a central headquarters. Reverend Leopold H. Tibesar, M.M., National Director for Japan, is planning the organization of a Superior Council for the whole country. In keeping with the Japanese Bishops' emphasis on social justice, the society will undertake the distribution of literature dealing with Catholic social principles, in addition to its regular program of charities.

Only charity on a vast scale can ameliorate conditions in Japan. The Catholic Church can establish conferences of St. Vincent de Paul and organize other charitable agencies. It can appeal for food and clothing from within the country and without. It can join hands with LARA (Licensed Agencies for Relief in Asia), the overall organization that supervises distribution of the contributions of American Catholic, Protestant, and civic agencies. And LARA, in turn, can repeat its 1946-1947 performance of distributing five million pounds of foodstuffs, clothing, and medicines. But charity, be it on a national or international scale, will not suffice to guarantee the existence of the Japanese people. Social justice must play its part, if we look for an equitable solution.

When all is said and done in the matter of charity, the stark fact remains that Japan is overpopulated. According to SCAP (Supreme Command of the Allied Powers), the country can not produce more than eighty per cent of the food necessary to meet minimum requirements. The normal situation is aggravated by the repatriation of six million additional persons from other lands. Until Japan's economy shall have been restored, international trade resumed, and emigration under United Nations auspices arranged, any substantial betterment of conditions will remain impossible.

During Japan's two centuries of self-imposed isolation, the nation had the same problem to face. The government resorted to a typically pagan solution—infanticide. Cold, calculated murder of the innocents kept the population stable in those days. Modern Japan is too Christian to entertain the idea of such a criminal solution of her difficulties. In her plight she turns to another Christian nation—the United States. And what does she receive? Some temporary succor, adulterated with Sangerist advice to the effect that her people decrease their birth rate in an immoral way. *"Domini est terra"*—"The earth is the Lord's, and the fullness thereof."

It is the height of stupidity to think that stagnant, if not dying, nations can continue to exclude more vigorous races from the sparsely settled areas of the world. The migration of peoples from overpopulated lands is a problem with which the United Nations must wrestle sooner or later. Until then, the national existence of Japan will always be precarious. We must reckon with the eventual reappearance of the samurai, if we shirk our responsibility in this matter.

In any event, Sangerism is not needed to decimate the population of Japan. Tuberculosis is doing that. Always a menace, this disease now stalks the land in the wake

194   NEW DAWN IN JAPAN

of the acute malnutrition of war. Associated with Japan's struggle to put an end to the ravages of tuberculosis, is the name of Father Joseph Flaujac, an old French missioner who, by reason of his constant concern with tubercular patients, has come to consider the disease as a personal enemy.

Father Flaujac, a veteran of almost forty years, first came in contact with the scourge of tuberculosis after the great earthquake of 1923. The sick coughing to death in the streets, tubercular persons committing suicide in despair, and the general lack of facilities to combat the "white plague"—all combined to fire Father Flaujac with the resolve to ameliorate the conditions of his adopted people. Six years later, this French missioner, who was practically penniless, opened a sanatorium in a rented house. In little more than a decade, he had built two large sanatoria, a preventorium, two rehabilitation centers, a home and school for the children of poor tubercular patients; and also had established a half-dozen dispensaries in and around Tokyo. In all these establishments, Father Flaujac is assisted by the native Sisterhood that he founded in 1931—the devoted Bernadettes. Unlike many of their race, these Japanese religious do not shrink from the service of tubercular patients.

So varied, however, are the physical needs of the Japanese people, that only a many-sided program of social activity can begin to do justice to the missioners' responsibility. During 1946 and 1947, the Catholic Church, despite its perennial poverty, inaugurated a magnificent series of new social works. Following is a comparative table that shows these recent social activities, as well as those of pre-war years. We are indebted to the March, 1948, issue of the *Missionary Bulletin* for this information.

CATHOLIC SOCIAL WORKS

	Pre-war	Post-war	Total
Kindergartens	58	11	69
Hospitals	9	4	13
Dispensaries	3	5	8
Orphanages	10	9	19
Nurseries	10	6	16
Homes for the Aged	7	2	9
Sanatoria	5	1	6
Repatriates' Homes	..	5	5
Homes for Girls	2	3	5
Other Establishments	2	2	4
TOTAL	106	48	154

It is regrettable that we may not pause longer in Tokyo to survey these various agencies of Christian charity. Before leaving the capital to continue our rapid survey of missions in Japan, the reader may be interested in a "look-see" at the latest in Catholic churches. Leave it to the "Yanks of the Orient" to think of this one! Even blasé New Yorkers would rub their eyes in disbelief, if one of their great department stores were to advertise: "Come to Macy's and go to Mass! Do your shopping afterwards!" Yet that is the kind of thing that has happened in downtown, down-to-earth Tokyo.

Mitsukoshi's—the capital's largest department store —remodeled its entire top floor into a Catholic chapel. This was blessed early in 1947, by Archbishop Peter Tatsuo Doi. Elevators now carry worshipers and curious alike to the seventh floor, where the operator blandly announces, "All out for the Catholic church!" There attendants are on hand daily to tell the tale of *Tenshu*. And Tokyo's biggest and busiest store is discovering that its top-floor chapel is a far better drawing card than its bargain basement.

Swinging northeast in a great arc, we come to Sendai, a city famous in missionary annals for the embassy sent by its daimio, Date (pronounced *Dahtay*), to the Pope and to the King of Spain in 1613. The Sendai mission is in care of Canadian Dominicans, who have made yeoman efforts to develop this corner of the Master's vineyard. Among recent advances is the latest project of the Christian Brothers—a Boys Town for Sendai, modeled on Father Flanagan's original foundation near Omaha, Nebraska. This establishment, which will not be completed until ten years hence, is planned to comprise an elementary school, a middle school, and a trade school, in addition to family-size houses that are designed to train the boys in practical home management. The Boys Town of Sendai is destined principally to take care of lads between the ages of fourteen and eighteen, who were orphaned by the war. It will serve, also, as an outlet for the orphanage conducted by the Dominican Sisters in Sendai.

Another wide arc to the north brings us to Aomori, at the tip of the main island. Across the Straits of Tsugaru, lies the island of Hokkaido, northernmost of the large islands of Japan's archipelago. Nippon made little serious effort to colonize this large island until early in the seventeenth century, when the feudal government of Ieyasu undertook to alienate the territory from the luckless Ainu, the aborigines of Japan. During this period of colonial exploitation, the Ainu were visited with shameless cruelty, every effort being made to deny them access to the arts of civilization. After the restoration of the Emperor, in 1868, the imperial government adopted a program of enlightened reforms in behalf of this remnant of an ancient people who in all probability originally belonged to the white race. Unfortunately, the process of deterioration had gone too far to save this mild and amiable people. The Ainu, Asia's ethnological question mark, seem destined to disappear.

Mention of feudal Japan's endeavor to perpetuate the ignorances of the Ainu reminds the author of a similar injustice perpetrated on a smaller scale by the Ainu among themselves. At the Shiraoi reservation during the summer of 1935, I visited the home of the headman of the tribe. At the moment he was out on "bear business," which is the biggest business in Ainu circles. In fact, the life of the Ainu revolves around the bear, which is hunted, worshiped, sacrificed, and eaten by them. While I was awaiting the headman's return, I had an opportunity to interview his wife. In the course of our conversation, I requested the amiable old lady to recite an Ainu prayer.

"Oh, sir," said she, "Ainu women never pray."

"Never pray!" I exclaimed. "All women pray."

"Not the Ainu women, sir. From time immemorial, our men have been careful to deny this knowledge to us women."

"And why?" I queried gently.

The old woman lowered her voice—there by the fireside beneath the pelt of a great brown bear.

"So that we should never be able, in moments of vexation, to call down upon their heads the punishment of Heaven."

As the gnarled old hands, so eloquent of the sufferings of our race, fumbled with the fire tongs, the inner meaning of that word "Ainu" came to me. Ainu means "Men," I thought, and this surely was a man's country, where even the women wore moustaches—tattooed on their upper lips. Very clever of us men! We would not let the women pray, lest they call down fire from heaven upon our guilty heads. But were we not a bit too clever for our own good? If women might not pray, they could not pray for us. And still, according to the revelations of Fatima, it is a woman—one peerless woman—who stands between us and the wrath of God!

When, the next day, I visited the Trappist monastery at Tobetsu, several hours distant by train from Hakodate, the port of Hokkaido, the significance of the old Ainu woman's remark struck me again. Out there in the rolling hills of Hokkaido, I came upon a group of strange, silent men on that island of strange fauna and strange hairy folk unknown to Japan. What were those silent, white-cowled hermits doing, so far from their native France? What had they been doing there, for sixty years and more? Making butter and cheese, which their rule did not permit them to eat? Suddenly it dawned on me, as I stood on the heights looking out to old ocean: those men were praying that never again should any child of woman be denied access to the truth that makes us free.

Due north is the diocese of Sapporo, confided to the care of the German Franciscans. It is enough to say that the Franciscans are interested in every department of missionary activity: churches, schools, hospitals, orphanages, foundling homes, printeries, and work for the blind.

Traveler, tarry long in the candlelight of Sapporo, for beyond this island of Hokkaido hangs an iron curtain that is not blowing into light. In Karafuto, on Sakhalin Island, the last candles of faith have been extinguished by atheistic communism of the Russian brand.

The Polish Franciscans, who labored valiantly though with little fruit, behind the iron curtain of Japanese militarism, may not labor there any more.

The iron curtain of Russian devising is much more impenetrable. But we know that the Soviet military authorities have taken over the mission station at Toichara, confining the missioners to the station of Otamari. The latter town, however, is a seaport, and the law does not permit foreigners to reside in such a strategic area. The unfortunate Poles have been refused permission to return to their own country; and since they will not be allowed to remain in Otamari, the only prospect for them seems to be work in the mines. The 557 Catholics in the prefecture will disappear: the Poles to Poland, and the Japanese to Nippon. But the missioners will stay *in testimonium fidei*—in witness to the Faith. And when the new iron curtain rusts away, as rust it must (for the proletariat will not be deceived forever), mayhap those brave men will be there, to light a taper unto the illumination of Sakhalin and the "Smoky Islands" to the north.

15. The Perils of Peace

CHRISTIAN DEMOCRACY, particularly as it is found in the United States, is the force that can make the most effective contribution to the spiritual rejuvenation of Japan. Never before has American prestige been so high in that unhappy land. We have taught the Japanese people an important lesson, which, unfortunately, they had to learn the hard way; namely, the lesson of their national waywardness. But now that they have learned it, the Japanese are grateful for the revelation.

Their country is ruined materially, but if such be the price of liberty, they will count it gain in the end. For the Japanese are not materialists. They will prize their spiritual emancipation above their material degradation. And in their logic, they will link their new-found liberties with America in two ways: they will look to our country, first, because they believe it to be great, and secondly, because they believe it to be decent.

In the eyes of the descendants of the samurai, we always shall be a great people, if for no other reason than that we succeeded in militarily defeating them. And we always shall be regarded by them as a decent people, because our conquering heroes proved anything but the vengeful monsters conjured up by their government-inspired propaganda.

Thus Nora Waln, in an article appearing in the *Saturday Evening Post*, reports a Japanese soldier, who had been in the battle of Singapore, as saying: "We respect you for beating us. We admire success. We know how hard we fought. It took wits, courage, and grit to bring us to unconditional surrender. As far as we are concerned in these northwestern valleys, it was the Americans who won the war. We expected you to occupy Japan and beat us into the earth. We were expecting rape, loot, starvation, and destruction. We would not have been surprised by any atrocity. Orientals commit atrocities when power is theirs. We were prepared to have you be crueler than ourselves, because we thought all Occidentals were barbarians."

The Japanese people see in our Christian democracy the secret of America's greatness and decency. They are looking to the United States for the development in their midst of a similar democracy. The United States, through the magnificent efforts of her representative—that providential person, General Douglas MacArthur—already has accomplished miracles in promoting the growth of Christian democracy in Japan. Consequently, the spiritual revolution now in progress in that country, a revolution that General MacArthur himself has characterized as without parallel in the social history of the world, has galvanized the enemies of democracy into a frenzy of counteractivity.

General MacArthur's administration of conquered

Japan never can be too highly praised. In the mature judgment of people who have lived, and are now living, in Japan, and who are cognizant of the realities of the situation, it would be a tragedy to nullify his endeavors. No heed should be given to the vicious mouthings of pseudo-Americans who would surrender Japan to the tyranny of Red fascism—a tyranny infinitely worse than Japan's recent militaristic dictatorship, under which the author lived for years.

General MacArthur, of course, did not start with a *tabula rasa* when he undertook the tutelage of the Japanese people. The seeds of democracy long had lain dormant in the soul of Japan. Even in feudal days, there were Japanese statesmen—like Koin Kido, for example —who were enamored of all that was best in the democratic system. But the heavy yoke of the slave-master tradition proved an insurmountable obstacle to the earlier democratization of their nation. In Japan, as in some other countries, there had been only a top and a bottom—with nothing between these two social extremes. The top always ruled. The rulers might change, as they did when, after the imperial restoration of 1868, the military clique combined with the vested interests; but the methods of rule never changed. Authority was always from above, never from below. The Japanese people, like every people imbruted and enslaved, were sick at heart. But, thank God, their sickness was never unto death.

The Japanese are group livers, rather than individualists. In their folkways, there is a rudimentary democracy, and they always have been careful to keep it alive. If the "neighborhood associations"—which the military perverted to their own ends in the pre-war years—were properly appraised, they could easily be integrated as factors in a democratic scheme of things. At any rate, in this group living of the Japanese people, there are the beginnings of self-government, which only need to be nurtured by political freedom.

The United States, as the principal occupying power, has afforded the Japanese people all the political freedom necessary for the success of the democratic revolution now going on in their midst. During the first year of the Occupation, the native military tyranny, hateful to many of the Japanese themselves, was destroyed utterly, though rather uneventfully. An army numbering some six million men was demobilized quietly; war criminals were removed from public life, and rounded up for trial; the vast economy of war was disassembled bit by bit, without prejudice to the people's minimum requirements. The beginnings of an industrial and commercial revival were encouraged. Moreover, the Japanese people were given a Bill of Rights, guaranteeing them the essential human freedoms. A new liberal Constitution was framed for them. The franchise was extended to women; the *zaibatsu*, or wealthy family-holding-companies, eighteen of which practically possessed Japan, were dissolved; a beginning was made in revamping the educational system, long a preserve of the military; and an enlightened program of land reform, intended to succor the down-trodden tenant farmer, was initiated.

Here was a pattern of reform truly herculean in its proportions. Upon such a course, only a people having the greatest faith in the democratic genius of the guiding authority would have embarked. The present progress of America's liberal program in Japan is at once a tribute to her own magnanimity, and a compliment to the caliber of the Japanese people, who have responded so well.

Presumably, the process of revolutionary adaptation that is now going on in Japan will require a lengthy period of trial and error, before we can hope for a complete, national adjustment. Certainly, Japan's nascent democracy must have ample opportunity to develop its sinews under favorable conditions. If left to its own resources too soon, it probably would succumb to the first vicious ism dynamic enough to spark a counterrevolution. A full-fledged democracy is the equal of any antagonist; we cannot reasonably expect that a nascent democracy, struggling to grow in an alien atmosphere, could cope with the brutal, cutthroat systems that have stamped out the first faint stirrings of democracy in other lands.

There is in Japan today a positive threat to the consummation of the democratic revolution that is so promising at present. This menace lies not so much in a growing reaction against many of the reforms contemplated by the Occupation authorities, nor in a possible resurgence of the recent (and ancient) militarism, as in the ultimate victory of communism. The latter is definitely in the field as a relentless competitor for the future of the Japanese people.

It is a well-known weakness of the democratic system that it must tolerate even the extreme opposition that plots democracy's destruction. Of course, there is, and should be, a limit to such toleration; but for the most part, democracy allows the individual to distinguish between the good and the bad, the true and the false. To deny the radical opposition a modicum of toleration, would be not democratic but fascistic—or what is the same thing, communistic. Therefore, in a democracy more than in any other political system, it is self-evident that "eternal vigilance is the price of liberty." This is especially true in regard to the nascent democracy of Japan, where the extreme opposition is intensely active in communism.

Japan, whether we care to admit the fact or not, is presently the battleground of two diametrically opposed ideologies—Christian democracy and atheistic communism. Unfortunately, it is still too early to predict the outcome of this epic struggle, which may affect the future not only of the whole Orient, but of the

whole world. But at present, at least, the communists
are a hundred times more active in Japan than are the
members of any other single political group.

These conclusions are supported by a recently published statement of James Monahan, formerly an intelli-
gence officer in the Far East Air Force. Said Mr. Monahan, writing for *The New York Times:*

"After the surrender, Japanese leaders familiar with
democratic processes were slow to emerge from the
shadows of totalitarian collapse. But another type of
leadership, trained for the opportunity, was readily
available. Release of political prisoners restored to activity the doctrinaire Communist group headed by
Kyuichi Tokuda. A few months later the Yenan group
of Communists, headed by Moscow-trained Sanzo Nozaka, was repatriated from Red China. As a result, the
Communists captured control of the new Japanese
labor movement, the radio, and the press."

Once they had established their hold on public
opinion, the Communists resorted to their usual smear
campaign. Everything that did not originate with themselves was either rotten or "reactionary." Democracy
of the American type was rotten, inasmuch as it favored
the rich employer rather than the poor worker. All
measures of social reform proposed by the Japanese
Government under the aegis of the American Supreme
Commander were unworthy of consideration, because
they were traceable to "reactionaries." On the other

hand, when Radio Siberia occasionally tired of disparaging General MacArthur and all things American, the least detail of Russian accomplishment was lauded to the skies, and "Soviet democracy"—a parody on the term, if ever there was one—was pictured to gullible Japanese as the only brand of liberalism for them.

Belated though our recognition of the insidious campaign of Asiatic communism has been, Americans are now awake to the situation, and have registered a reaction. Henceforth, we will be on the alert to safeguard our democratic accomplishments and commitments. But unfortunately, the damage that has been done is serious, and it calls for positive countermeasures on our part.

The Communists, by their early monopoly of the avenues of public opinion, have poisoned many a mind. Regrettably, the end of this poisoning process is not yet, for the oceans of literature with which Communists flooded the book stores are capable of deceiving many more people. "*Scriptum manet.*" Not long ago, seventy per cent of all the literature on sale in some of Japan's great cities was communistic. At the same time, there was a dismaying dearth of printed matter suitable to be utilized as an antidote.

As genuine Americans, believing in the fundamental verities and virtues of our Christian democracy, imperfect though it still may be, we cannot remain indifferent to the inroads of atheistic communism in Japan.

Americans have a stake in Japan's destiny. Every country lost to the cause of Christian democracy is another nail in our own collective coffin. The "overwhelming state," to use the words of columnist George Sokolsky, does not tolerate the man who seeks to live his own life.

As Catholics, we find the spread of atheistic communism—and it is always atheistic—in Japan, as everywhere else, a vital issue, one with life-and-death implications for us. It is high time that we abandoned our smug assurance in the belief that we belong to a powerful religious group, which is unassailable on every side. We are not only smug, but stupid. Ours is now the most persecuted religion in the world. Eighty million or more European Catholics, who once were living in a world of seeming security, are now living in a communistic empire, where the practice of their Faith is not tolerated.

Some American Catholics may think that communism's victory in Japan can have no vital bearing on our own security. Smugness and stupidity again! A long-range view of the situation indicates that Japan will be the pivotal country of Asia for a long time. As Japan will go, so other Asiatic countries will be bound to go. If, therefore, communism triumphs in Japan, it certainly will not stop there. Crusading religion that it is, it will threaten all Asia sooner or later.

"But," you may say, "it can't happen here!"

"Why not?" I ask.

"Because there are no signs of such a revolution."

"Ah, so that is it! No signs of a coming revolution? Communism does not come necessarily by way of revolution. Where revolution is possible, communism elects that avenue of approach; but where it is not possible, communism comes by way of attrition. That is the way it is slashing the fabric of Japan—and the way by which it would like to penetrate the fiber of America."

Hitoshi Ashida, the present Premier of Japan, in a public statement pledged that his administration would take "determined steps" to curb unrest harmful to the reconstruction of his country. The Premier openly charged that "certain elements" were exerting "a baneful influence" in order to disrupt Japanese industry. Although he did not mention the Communists by name, it is well understood that he was referring to the Communist party, which, though numerically small, exerts a disproportionate influence in the new labor unions.

Recently Japanese labor has begun to manifest signs of dissatisfaction. The unions dare not undertake any demonstration tantamount to a general strike, because such action would entail swift intervention by the Occupation authorities. But they initiate temporary stoppages, even in key industries, and thus succeed in partly paralyzing the forces of reconstruction. This potential labor unrest, inspired and exacerbated by the Communists, is bound to become one of the greatest problems that will beset our Occupation forces in Japan.

Not long ago, Tatsuo Tanaka, Governor of Yama-guchi Prefecture, stated that, in his opinion, two thirds of all trade union members in Yamaguchi were Communists. Communist propaganda, he said, was making headway, also, among farmers' unions, farm co-opera-tives, and fishermen's organizations. So important is the Yamaguchi branch of the Communist party in the eyes of the overlords in Tokyo, that Sanzo Nozaka, Japan's top Communist, makes frequent visits to Yamaguchi, the place where he was born.

Mr. Tanaka told Lindesay Parrot, a reporter for *The New York Times,* that he believes his prefecture is the Number One target of Japanese Communists, on ac-count of its proximity to Korea. Small fishing boats cross the straits from Russian-occupied Korea in nine hours. The crews of those boats smuggle into Yamaguchi, the nearest point in Japan, numerous Communist agents, who are soon lost among the fifty thousand Koreans. Governor Tanaka believes that the Occupation author-ities should take "positive action" against the Com-munists, outlawing their subversive party if necessary.

"Relations are plainly worsening between the United States and the Soviet Union," said Governor Tanaka to the *New York Times* reporter. "The United States, because of its distance from the scene of possible con-flict, and its great power, probably can afford to allow the Communists to operate openly. But this is a luxury that is not for the Japanese placed directly in the path of conflict. . . . The Occupation is mistaken in permitting Japanese Communists openly to solicit members and spread propaganda. If outlawing the Japanese Communist party drives it underground, it will be weaker than it is today."

We may not agree fully with Governor Tanaka's ideas, but we can not gainsay the logic of his contention that something should be done to meet the terrible urgency of the situation. It would be a tragic error to permit ourselves to enjoy a false sense of security, simply because the Communists in Japan have not attempted by any overt act to disturb the *status quo*. They have not attempted to do so, because they dare not do so. For the moment, and probably for the length of the Occupation, they will be content to support the advances of the Socialist party; but once the Allied forces quit Japan, we may expect positive action on the part of the Communists. At present the red beast sleeps—but with one eye open.

To be a true democracy or a Soviet vassal state, is the choice now offered to Japan. To inspire and support the right choice, there is only the United States of America. Woe to Japan, and woe to us, if the United States does not stand fast!

16. A Program for the Dawn

WHAT SHOULD BE our defense against the spread of communism in Japan? Exactly what it is here in our own country: enlightenment in the intellectual order, and practical justice and charity in the social order.

First must come enlightenment. The Japanese people must be disabused of many of their alleged ideals. But since they will need something to take the place of what we ask them to surrender, they must be taught a new and true idealism. This implies a positive program of education, one involving the solution of essential psychological and spiritual problems. This is where religion must make its contribution, and any attempt to settle the issue to the exclusion of religion must be foredoomed to failure.

Japan's enlightenment must come (a) by word of mouth, and (b) by the printed word. *By word of mouth,* the truth that will free the soul of Japan must reach her through the instrumentality of Christian missioners, before all others. Statesmen will be necessary; teachers, too, and experts of every kind; but the first need is Christian missioners. Why? Simply because the missioner's status is understood and approved. He is a certified individual; whereas, all others are suspect until they, like him, have proved themselves. *By the printed word*, the truth will enlighten the mind of Japan if we provide the proper literature. The prevailing paper shortage, and the consequent lack of reading along the right lines is, one must admit, little short of disastrous for the future of Japan. What can be done to ease the situation? Print good books by the thousands, and send them to key persons in Japan, if not to many others! Thus will be made possible the spread of enlightenment by the Japanese themselves.

During the war, Americans mobilized millions of men and billions of dollars, in order to defeat a wicked philosophy. The job is done—unless we, at this late hour, suffer it to be undone by the equally vicious philosophy of communism, which has raised its ugly head for the second time in Japan. Shall we now refuse to consummate our task by sending to the Japanese people a few hundred certified representatives, and a few thousand certified books?

Secondly, Japan's enlightenment must be complemented, in the social order, by a practical program of Christian justice and charity. Today everybody realizes that there has been an evolution in social thinking and action. However much this evolution may disconcert certain Christians, it offers no challenge to Christianity —which is a notably practical religion. The uplifting of humanity spiritually, mentally, morally, emotionally, socially, and esthetically—in short, the regeneration of the whole man—is the mission of Christianity.

The true follower of Christ, while holding fast to individual, religious, and civic liberty, is in favor of everything that practically and progressively enhances the welfare of the masses of the people everywhere. But a non-Christian people, such as the Japanese, has to be convinced of this. A vigorous apostolate of Christian social action, then, must be our second line of defense against communism. In the light of the social gospel of Christ, communism will appear to the Japanese as the fraud that it is.

The United States, then, must tackle and settle the Japanese problem in a spirit of Christian and democratic fair play. We have made a splendid beginning, as the Japanese themselves admit. Premier Ashida, on the occasion of his installation in March of 1948, expressed "the nation's profound gratitude" for an occupation policy "executed with a spirit of benevolence and generosity unparalleled in history." This American policy of Christian and democratic decency, however, must be further articulated in a practical way, as rapidly as conditions will permit.

Japan needs economic stability. This means that the United States, as principal occupying power, must first clarify its policy in regard to the rebuilding of Japanese industry, without which there can be no true economic stability. Until this clarification is realized, Japan cannot utilize her own resources to the utmost degree. Thus, she must continue her present food imports on a credit basis, and that is not a salutary situation.

Japan suffers from the threat of inflation. In order to combat this danger, increased production must be encouraged by giving priorities to key industries. The development of small and medium business enterprises of all kinds must be fostered, in an effort to stimulate the export and tourist trades. Such a program calls for active co-operation on the part of the Occupation authorities. And it implies the necessity of financial aid, which can be realized only through private loans, inasmuch as national sentiment probably is still too sensitive to encourage public grants. No Japanese statesman has dared to mention the need of commercial credits in the rebuilding of Japan's economy; but this is certainly a problem that must be faced sooner or later—at least by individuals who are willing to invest.

Material assistance, however, will not be sufficient to tide Japan over this crisis. The Japanese people are in need of moral support, also. They look to Americans for that leadership which many of their own statesmen have denied them. Among officials who are co-operating with the Occupation authorities, there are many pre-war administrators who lack the ability to convince the Japanese people of the merits and the benefits of democracy. Consequently, it devolves upon us to further the education and promotion to high public office of democratic-minded Japanese, in whose hands the future of the present democratic revolution will be secure in all its political and social phases.

But how, it may be asked, dare we Americans hope to accomplish in an alien civilization what we have not thoroughly achieved in our homeland? How can we expect to bring about the political and social betterment of the Japanese masses, when we have contributed little to the social salvation of many of our own countrymen? Ah, we are vulnerable there! Truly, we lack the aggressive determination, the enterprising dynamism, the persistent activity, of the Communists. While they are rapidly sweeping over the whole world, we disciples of Christ—the first great social reformer—are lagging far behind in social initiative.

Thank God, we are at least in the race, slow though our progress has been. At long last we are awake to the social problem, in all its world-wide ramifications. At last we are beginning to bestir ourselves in solving it. Fortunately, we shall be able to make up lost time, because ours is a blueprint of action, complete and infallible, bequeathed to us by God Himself. On the other hand, the Communists are bound to lose time experimenting, as they must, with a plan of action riddled with the shortcomings and inconsistencies of all things human.

In the meantime, while we are struggling ahead of them in measures of world-wide, social uplift, let us not permit them to steal our thunder. Christ, not Marx, was the first to champion the interests of the downtrodden. Christ, not Marx, was the only one who died to save mankind. And many of the reforms that the followers of Marx are demanding in behalf of the proletariat, are the very things that Jesus Christ championed long centuries ago. Therefore, let us not suffer these upstarts in social reform to take credit for the accomplishments of Christianity. Let us work for the advent of that happy day of achievement in our own land, if nowhere else, when we shall be able to face that little clique of clever bureaucrats who batten and fatten on social unrest, dismaying them with our "baptized" version of the "Internationale:"

"Arise, ye victims of starvation;
    Arise, ye wretched from your birth;
For Jesus Christ through tribulation
    Has made of you the salt of earth.

"We who were brutes for generations,
    Are now no longer slaves in thrall.
This earth shall rise on new foundations;
    Once we were naught, who now are all!

Chorus

" 'Tis the final conflict—
    Let each one take his place.
The brotherhood of Jesus Christ
    Salutes the human race."

True, much remains to be done in our own country, before the ideals of the social gospel of Christ will be realized in full. But we have succeeded in making some progress toward that objective. This measure of social achievement we are asked to share with the people of Japan.

The effective motivation of such an enlightened program of practical social justice as that which democratic Americans propose for Japan, can come only from the Christian religion. That religion is the wellspring of all our fundamental democratic principles. Since Christianity is at once the progenitor and protector of our democracy, and since it alone offers any persistent and serious opposition to the inroads of Red fascism, communism's ruthless persecution of the Christian religion is understandable. In Japan, as elsewhere, the Communist party aims first and foremost at the destruction of Christianity—deny it though Communists may.

Says Moscow-trained Sanzo Nozaka, leader of the Japanese Communists, in a masterpiece of understatement: "We are materialists. Our goal is to make religion disappear." It is the Communist in Nozaka, rather than the Japanese in him, who gives expression to this irreligious resolve, for the Japanese people are not materialists. And when Comrade Nozaka speaks about the disappearance of religion, he is not thinking of Buddhism or Shinto: he refers to Christianity, by which he means the Catholic religion.

Such, then, is the unsubtle challenge hurled at us Christians by Moscow's puppet in Japan: "Communism

—or else!" Whether we in the the United States will it or not, Christianity is being taken into consideration in the monumental transformation of the life of New Japan. It is being considered by those who love Christian democracy; and, perhaps, even more by those who hate it. But at present the vast majority of the Japanese people do not appear eager to uphold communism. On the contrary, they are more inclined to uphold Christianity and Christian democracy. They realize their need of our political experience; and they look to us for spiritual succor, also, in the matter of religion. Admiring all things American, they naturally turn to the religion of the United States, hoping therewith to fill their great spiritual void.

Hitherto, Christianity has made poor visible progress in Japan. What, indeed, shall we say of the enormous dedication of human life, and the not-inconsiderable expenditure of material resources, thus far involved in the missionary movement in that country, in view of the apparently insignificant results? In this year of 1948, in which are met all the blood and sweat and tears shed through all the years since Saint Francis Xavier carried the Gospel to the Sunrise Kingdom, the total practising Christian membership—Catholic and non-Catholic combined—hardly aggregates one-half of one per cent of the population. Shall we say, then, that the missionary program in Japan is justified?

No one should know better than the foreign mis-

sioner who has to do the grubbing in the field afar, and
he does not hesitate to answer the question affirmatively.
The foundation for his opinion is the fact that the
Christian influence in Japan cannot be reckoned by
mere statistical tables. Such data never can plot the inroads of the Gospel into the cultural and social life of
the Japanese people, any more than they can reveal the
count of those who belong to the soul, rather than the
body, of the Church. While it is true that the general
permeation of Christian ideas in Japan is attributable to
the Church, it does not follow that the active membership of organized Churches embraces all that is Christian
in Japanese society today.

This is a point that should be emphasized: Japan is
much more Christian than one would deduce from
tables of statistics. The leaven of the Gospel long has
been astir in the paste of that island people, who in spite
of all the obloquy visited upon their heads by a world
aghast at the atrocities of their armies, are soul-hungry
today, and sincerely desirous of sharing in our Christian
Faith. They do not fail to see the excellence and beauty
of that Faith, even though it is professed by their former
enemy.

There is, however, a visible progress in the Christianization of Japan, and this can be tabulated. The official
statistics for 1944 showed a total enrollment of approximately 120,000 Catholics. There were also about
50,000 Greek Orthodox believers, and approximately

200,000 Protestants of all denominations. These figures give a modest grand total of approximately 370,000 Christians, in a population of about 75,000,000; but actually the total figures may have been closer to 350,-000 believers.

Almost 10,000 Catholics "went to heaven" in 1945, when an atom bomb desolated the holy city of Nagasaki. This, certainly, was a tragedy, the memory of which the people of the United States should strive to efface by rebuilding the venerable church in Urakami as a tribute to those who perished within the shadow of its spires. The cornerstone of the new church should bear a fitting inscription to the effect that the atom bomb had not been aimed at this settlement of our Christian brethren, but had been diverted from its course by bad weather.

Probably another 10,000 Catholics were lost to the Faith in consequence of wartime defections, migrations, and deaths.

The ravages of the war can be reckoned in a general way by a recent report of the Rehabilitation Committee of the Catholic Church in Japan. According to this report, Catholics numbered 119,262 in 1939; but they totaled only 112,285 in 1947, although that year witnessed more than 4,000 adult baptisms. In the same report, a comparative table of statistics for the years 1939, 1946, and 1947 shows that while adult baptisms decreased to 1,394 in 1946, as compared with 1,732 in

1939, they rose to 4,048 in 1947. Catechumens numbered only 2,573 in 1939; but they jumped to 9,047 in 1946; and to 10,788 in 1947.

As in the case of the Catholic laity, the ranks of the clergy, too, were depleted during the course of the war. About fifteen per cent of the priests in Japan were interned, or later repatriated in an exchange of internees during the summer of 1942. The majority of these missioners are back again at their stations, in a demonstration of Christian loyalty and devotion that has not been lost upon the Japanese people. One bishop was murdered, when he demanded the restitution of his cathedral after it had been confiscated by the military. One priest died in prison; four others met death in air raids, not to mention the casualties sustained in the armed forces.

At present, there are more than 300 foreign priests and 164 native priests laboring in Japan. They are assisted by more than 272 Brothers (of whom 187 are Japanese) and 2,031 Sisters (more than half of whom are Japanese), all working in one way or another to make New Japan Christ-conscious.

This missionary personnel, which totals 2,781, represents 17 religious communities of men, and 43 religious communities of women (11 of them entirely Japanese). Among these foreign missioners, the recent report of the Rehabilitation Committee of the Catholic Church in Japan tabulates 25 separate national and ethnical groups. The totals are: Germans, 201; French, 172; Canadians, 122; Italians, 96; Americans, 61; Spanish, 41; Irish, 29; Polish, 22; Australians, 20; Koreans, 19; Belgians, 18; English, 11; Swiss, 11; Chinese, 7. The last named are all nuns.

Malta is represented by 6 missioners; Argentina and Austria by 5 each; Czechoslovakia and Holland by 4 each; Portugal by 3; New Zealand, Croatia, Hungary, and Luxembourg by 2 each; Lithuania by one.

We cannot detail here the many-sided activity of this missionary League of Nations, except to say that by 1941 the Japanese Catholic Church was maintaining, in addition to approximately 300 houses of worship, an educational system comprising the following: 16 theological schools, (major and minor); one university and one college; 5 junior colleges; 40 high schools; 12 commercial schools; 12 primary schools; 85 kindergartens. The Church maintained, also, a social-service organization embracing approximately the following: 30 hospitals, sanatoria, and dispensaries; 8 hostels; 6 settlement houses; 30 orphanages and old folks' homes; 20 nurseries. As a result of the devastations of war, this inspiring picture of Catholic missionary zeal has undergone a complete transformation.

In addition to losses in personnel, the Catholic Church in wartime Japan has suffered serious material disabilities. Estimates of damage to property of the Catholic Church alone run between $5,000,000 and

$10,000,000. Air raids destroyed 72 churches (one fifth of all the mission stations), most of them located in urban centers. In Tokyo alone, 11 out of 18 churches, including the old cathedral at Sekiguchi, are in ruins. Besides, many school and monastery chapels have disappeared in the capital. More than half of the Catholic school buildings in the principal cities have met the same fate.

It is more difficult to assess the losses incurred by the Protestant churches in Japan. In regard to personnel, Protestants, like Catholics, died in air raids at home, as well as in the ranks of the armed services. Protestants, like Catholics, suffered wartime defections. Among Protestants, however, these defections were much more numerous, owing not only to the loose-knit organization and general doctrinal confusion of Protestantism, but especially to the deterioration which resulted from compulsory membership in the legal corporation known as the "United Church of Christ in Japan."

The material losses inflicted on Protestant institutions have reached a staggering total. Richard Terrell Baker, who recently made a detailed study of the hardships experienced by the Christian Church in wartime Japan, tells us in his book, *Darkness of the Sun,* that 455 of the 1,600 Protestant churches in the country were damaged or destroyed. More than 300 parsonages of Protestant ministers, he says, also went up in smoke. Schools and welfare institutions of every kind lie buried beneath the rubble that clutters the great cities of Nippon. Only in Kyoto, the one major city exempted from bombing by the United States Army Air Forces, the Christian churches and auxiliary institutions, both Catholic and Protestant, remain undamaged. Truly, the losses visited on Protestant evangelical, educational, social, and medical establishments will be felt for decades to come.

If Japan is ever to recover from the disastrous effects of World War II, she must receive substantial help. To say, as some have said, that her people should "stew in their own juice" is a short-sighted policy, indeed; one that can only result in the loss of a nation to the cause of Christian decency. The people of the United States must resolve to be the spiritual saviors of these 80,000,000 souls who now cannot help themselves.

To be sure, we can neglect this epic opportunity for world-leadership and relegate the Japanese people, in the most paralyzing disaster ever to befall their nation, to the slough of despond. But if we choose to do so, let us be prepared to stultify ourselves, because the Japanese inevitably will turn to succor either to the right or to the left—either to the samurai disguised as arch-conservatives, or to the Communists self-styled the saviors of the outcast. In either eventuality, we shall have lost the Pacific war (as we already appear to have lost the European war), and the sacrifice of our heroic youth will have been in vain.

17. The Eagle and the Sun

In the midst of their desolation, the Japanese are looking to the people of the United States, not so much for a material endowment of church, school and social service facilities to replace those that they have lost, as for a spiritual enrichment by American missioners, who will bless them with the consolations of the Gospel. The Japanese people are longing for the truth of Christ, and they are turning to us, of all people, for this gift exceedingly great.

Doctor Kotaro Tanaka, that brilliant Catholic philosopher, who was in eclipse under the rule of the jingoes, speaks for his fellow countrymen: "In the missions of American Catholics, we discover this living force of Christianity in the United States. . . . Let us tie between the Catholics of our two nations stronger bonds than existed in the past, when far too few American missioners were amongst us."

Unfortunately, it is only too true that American Catholics in the past have overlooked Japan in their missionary activities. Except for the Sisters of Notre Dame de Namur (at Okayama), and the Maryknoll Fathers and Maryknoll Sisters (in Kyoto), there were no strictly American Catholic foundations laboring in Japan proper during pre-war years; although some

Americans had been loaned to European groups laboring there. Happily, the post-war picture is changing in
this respect. There is good reason to believe that at
least six more American communities will engage in
missionary work in Nippon within the next few years.
Among these new recruits may be mentioned, besides
the American Capuchins, Oblates of Mary Immaculate,
and Franciscan Friars of the Atonement, the Viatorians
and the School Sisters of Notre Dame. The two latter
communities are planning to undertake educational
work in the Maryknoll mission of Kyoto, in central
Japan.

American Catholics may be surprised to learn that
there are Japanese who regard their lack of interest as
nothing short of a betrayal. The author remembers an
incident that occurred shortly before his repatriation,
in 1942, which brought this home to him very force-
fully. He was standing on the dock in Yokohama, after
having been "processed" preparatory to going aboard
the exchange ship, *Asama Maru*. A Japanese professor
approached one of the author's companions, whom he
had known before the outbreak of hostilities, and asked
to have a few words with him. The record of this conversation—one of the strangest attacks on the Catholic
Church that the missioner encountered during his years
in Japan—we owe to the excellent reporting of
Reverend James G. Keller, M.M., in his recent volume,
The Priest and a World Vision.

"I have been studying your religion," said the Japanese professor, who was not a Christian, "and I am convinced that its philosophy of life could bring lasting peace to all nations. But you have not fulfilled the command of your Founder, Jesus Christ. He bade you bring His teaching, His Gospel, to all men of all nations. You Catholics have not done this. And you are not even making a serious attempt to do it now.

"Take my country, for instance. We have 80,000,000 people. But you who preach that you are interested in *all* men have only a few hundred priests here. There is need for thousands. When the Nazis got an opening to bring their ideas into our country, within a very short time they dispatched nearly 4,000 technicians to Japan. Their business was to be emissaries of the Nazi philosophy, as well as to help strengthen our war machines.

"During the last thirty years, we Japanese have been looking for a new way of life. We went to America, and what did we get? Automobiles, machines, movies, radio! But that was not enough. We tried England, and England offered a strong caste system, on the one hand, and industrialization of the masses, on the other. We turned to the Russians, who gladly gave us Karl Marx. Personally, I don't think his philosophy of life offers any permanent solution.

"During the past years, I have been studying the Catholic Church, and the pattern of life it proposes. And I have come to the conclusion that, if it were only workable, it would furnish the solution of all mankind's difficulties, and would establish world peace and happiness. But you don't take your own Faith seriously.

"I am afraid it is too late for us to change. We are now in a war to the death, and it is impossible to turn back. Some of us realize our terrible mistake. But nothing can be done about it now. All I wish to convey to you, as you are leaving my country, is that your Church could have prevented Japan from embarking on this unfortunate program of war, which is based on false and mistaken ideas. But I blame you, because you Catholics had the truth, and yet made little more than a gesture to bring it to our 80,000,000 people.

"I feel you have cheated us. But I hope you will not make this same mistake again, in any other part of the world."

Oh, American Catholics! What a tribute, what a plea, what a challenge to your Faith, is this reproach of an earnest Oriental: "You have cheated us."

A Christian America could Christianize Japan, if only it were willing to undertake the task with so much as half of the determination, persistency, and devotion with which Communists are secretly striving for the mastery of that unhappy land. Japan is a small, compact country (less than the size of California in area), with a homogeneous people, who are all acquainted—superficially, at least—with Christianity. Is it, therefore, unreasonable to think that this close-knit nation, interlaced with family ties that are among the strongest in the world, might be largely Christianized, if the people of America would devote themselves sincerely to such an undertaking?

If Japan, with her genius for initiative, efficiency, persistency, and drive, should be Christianized even in part, what incalculable possibilities would be opened up for the conversion of all the teeming millions of the Orient! Most of those millions are now alien to all that is best in Christian civilization.

From time immemorial, except during the years of enforced isolation, the Japanese has been the *ronin* —the "wave man," or wanderer—of the Far East. Restless with the pulse of his ancestral seas, he has ranged up and down the vast Orient for centuries. And he will do so always: to this he is predestined by the spirit in his blood. Wherever the Japanese has gone, he has carried with him his household deities, from which he cannot be detached. If, then, this Aeneas of the East should be won to Christ, might he not become to other Orientals, if only by his Christian deportment, a harbinger of that Light to which so many of us Occidentals have grown purblind?

How roseate the Christian future of Japan will be, we dare not prophesy. Greater seers have failed in this, particularly when, in the middle of the nineteenth century, some confidently predicted the speedy conversion of Japan to Christianity. What the future will hold, we cannot say, unless we may gauge its promise from the present. Japan's present, indeed, is rich in great opportunities. But we should be rash to make this fact the premise of a prophecy, because opportunities are more easily neglected than seized. How applicable this truth is in regard to the Christianization of Japan!

The opportunity of winning to Christ at least a sizable proportion of this island nation, although neglected in the past, is offered again—and this time, if not heretofore, to Americans. We are the people, among all in the world, who can best take advantage of the opportunity, and thus influence the destiny of Japan. As far as American Catholics are concerned, a beginning has been made. But it is only a beginning. Although Japan is presently divided into fifteen ecclesiastical provinces (comprising one archbishopric, five dioceses, two vicariates apostolic, and seven prefectures apostolic), American priests, Brothers, and Sisters are working in very few of them.

To young Catholic America, in the person of the Catholic Foreign Mission Society of America (Maryknoll), the Holy See in 1933 awarded the mission field of Kyoto. This is located in the central part of Honshu, Japan's main island. The mission, which is only a small portion of a territory about the size of the State of Kansas, is, nevertheless, important, because it embraces the civil prefecture of Kyoto, the center of Japanese Buddhism; and also Nara, the center of Shintoism, and Omi (Shiga County), once a thriving center of Catholicism in sixteenth-century Japan. Especially in Kyoto, the ancient capital, is given to the missioners of Maryknoll the privilege of following in the footsteps of Saint Francis Xavier, and the courage to dare where he, great apostle, is humanly thought to have failed.

Maryknoll has its full pre-war complement of priests, Brothers, and Sisters, at work again in Japan, and recruits have joined them. But all the missioners whom Maryknoll can commission for Japan will be far too few to garner even that portion of the precious harvest assigned to them.

From the United States, many more apostolic laborers are needed for the mission of Japan—men and women who will not be slow to forsake the highways for the byways. Missioners are needed, of course, for the apostolate of the cities, where the Christian Church long has made its strongest appeal to the professional and upper, middle-class groups. But it is especially in the rural areas, among the debt-ridden farming and laboring classes who live precariously from hand to mouth, that the followers of Christ must make their stand in New Japan.

There, in the hinterlands, among the poor and under-privileged, is the trysting place of our Christian democratic civilization and the new barbarism of atheistic communism. To the downtrodden multitudes of the hinterland (whose voice is not heard in the councils of urban labor unions) must the apostles of our generation carry the Gospel of Christ, in all its social implications, and with the greatest dispatch at their command, lest those millions whose courage is small rise in the might of their wrath and wreck the last best hope of Christian civilization by gravitating toward the mirage of atheistic communism. Moods of weariness, disillusionment and despair will hardly predispose the Japanese people for acceptance of the Christian religion. *"Hana yori dango"* —"A dumpling rather than a flower!" Did not Our Lord Jesus give bread to the multitudes who sought Him for the word of life?

In Japan the fields are white again—white for the third, and mayhap the last time! As Father Patrick J. Byrne declared, upon his return to the United States for a temporary respite after long internment in Japan: "The Maryknoll missioners simply are overwhelmed with requests for instruction. We are teaching the catechism from early morning until late at night."

This might be called an echo of the statement made by a nun in Tokyo to Bishop O'Hara of Buffalo when, on a visit to Japan last year, that prelate inquired if many Japanese were manifesting a desire for instruction in the Faith. The nun replied: "Every day they come to the gate of our convent, ring the bell, and say, 'Please teach me Christ!' "

The harvest, then, is ripe—riper than it has ever been before. And laborers are needed to glean those sheaves of precious souls—particularly laborers from America, because the Japanese people naturally turn to us for guidance at a time when this country has assumed the chief burden of their regeneration. American Catholics, by reason of the unity of their Faith, are, in the words of Doctor Kotaro Tanaka, the best representatives of American Christianity.

The author voices this opinion without the least animus. Although, on occasion, he has encountered Protestant missionaries in whose minds evangelization was identified with denunciation of the Catholic Church, the missionary zeal of the vast majority of our Separated Brethren is too sincere to merit anything but the highest respect. Still, it is a fact which one must recognize in simple honesty that Protestantism, because of the variety and multiplicity of its creeds, has slowed the clock of Japan's conversion to the Christian faith. The disunited front which Christianity presents is a scandal to us here at home, and it can only be a source of genuine bewilderment to the people in mission lands. Christ, our Master, said, "There shall be one flock and one shepherd." How dare we, then, gainsay Him?

In spite of this monumental tragedy of disunion, may God grant that the consequences of Japan's great spiritual hunger will be vast and stimulating, at least as far as American Christians are concerned. And woe to us, if we suffer not the love of Christ Crucified to achieve for our two nations a rapprochement more genuinely sincere and enduring than that which was forced upon us by the cosmic violence of the atom bomb.

It is the spirit of Christianity to forgive and forget. When the Japanese people were bent upon aggression and disturbance of the peace, we refused to co-operate with them, and rightly so. But now all is changed. Nippon's feet are set in peaceful ways. She is the one bright spot in all the territories that the United States now occupies. And her former rising sun has set—to shine upon a better day. Good! Now our eagle may rejoice again, for he always loved the sun.

If evidence means anything, we can be sure that the present progress of the Japanese people is along the path of international decency and universal fellowship. Shall we, then, in our impassioned desire to win the peace and prevent a future war, refuse the co-operation of the Japanese in the interests of a Christian, democratic world, simply because their co-operation is belated? This American, who himself was interned early in the war and, with many Japanese, suffered at the hands of the instigators of that conflict, cries, "No!"

Quench not the smoking flax! Crush not the broken reed! To say, "We forgive," is Christian. To say, "Okay, forget it! Let's start all over again," is American. To say or do otherwise would be irrational, provocative, undemocratic, un-American, un-Christian.

Yes, it would be tantamount to unhallowing, if such a thing were possible, the sainted sacrifice of our soldier-dead, who so magnanimously poured out the crimson libation of their youthful lives for the assurance of a better world.

Index

annihilation of Shimabara Christians, 47

EAGLE, AMERICAN, 143, 227, 236
Eastern Lodge, 127, 129, 136, 140, 146
Ecclesiastical divisions, 71
Economy, wartime, 92
Education, Christian primary, 169; Japanese, excessive specialization of, 171; need of religious, 170; religious, State participation in, 166; revamped, 205; State monopoly of primary, 169
Educational policy, of Japanese Government, 74; of post-war Japan, 166
Educational system, revamping of, 205
Emancipation, of Buddhism, 76; of Christian schools, 168; of Christianity (1873), 71; of Christianity, 76; of Shinto, 76; of shrines and temples, 12; religious, 168
Embassy to Pope (1582), 39
Embassy to Pope and King of Spain, 196
Emigration, 193
Emperor, Japanese, 139, 161; a *living deity*, 95; abject status of, 26, 36; bravery of, 161; cult of, 95; denial of divinity of, 121; divinity of, 6, 94, 95; in hiding, 161; not divine in Christian sense, 95; repudiation of divinitv by, 10; restoration of, 9, 197, 203; surrender proclamation of, 160, 161; victimized by military, 10, 11, 161
English philosophy, 76
English traders, 46
Enigma of the West, 45, 75, 77, 79, 80, 178
Episcopalians, 72
Estrangement from West, psychological, 58
Evacuees, aboard *Gripsholm*, 155; exchanged in East Africa, 152; hostility among, 153; morale, 151; physical condition of, 152
Exclusion Acts, American, 159; Japanese, 57
Exclusion of foreigners, 57

FAGE, PÈRE JOSEPH, M.E., 80, 81, 82
Farming class, in feudal Japan, 53; land reform in favor of, 205; target of Communistic propaganda, 211
Fascism, red, 219

Fatima, 199
Felsecker, Rev. Harold, M.M., 182
Fernandez, Brother John, S.J., 20, 22, 24, 31
Feudal strife, 26, 36, 37
Fillmore, President, 66
Flag, American, 124, 125, 143, 150, 151
Flanagan, Father, 189
Flaujac, Rev. Joseph, M.E., 194
Forcade, Father, 60, 61
Foreign missioners, 173; deportation of, 48; mistakes of, 46; self-sacrifice of, 22, 31, 32; unjust jailing of, 103
Food, importation of, 216; insufficient production of, 192; lack of, 114, 115, 132, 135, 178
Forward Island, 65
Francis Xavier, St., 16, 68, 69, 115, 185, 220; apostolate in Bungo, 32; apostolate in Hirado, 23, 24; apostolate in Kagoshima, 20; apostolate in Kyoto, 25-27; apostolate in Yamaguchi, 24, 28; apostolic strategy of, 177; apostolic zeal of, 19, 20, 22-24, 29; deification of, 177; en route to Kyoto, 25, 26; failure in Kyoto, 26; holiness of, 21; last visit to Goa, 31, 32; linguistic ability of, 21, 22; memorial to, 80, 177; mission strategy of, 20, 24, 26, 27, 30, 32; monument to, 28; spoliation of shrine of, 176; successes of, 22, 28, 29; successors of, 31; wartime apostolate of, 176, 177
Franciscan Friars of the Atonement, 180
Franciscan Missionaries of Mary, 180, 181
Franciscans, Canadian, 174; German, 74, 199; Japanese, 43; Polish, 200; Spanish, 38, 42, 43
Froez, Father, S.J., 32
Fukuin Maru, 83
Fukuoka, 43
Funay, college and university of, 32
Furuya, Monsignor Paul, 183; Mr. and Mrs., 81

G.I.'S, AMERICAN CATHOLIC, 13
Gervasi, Frank, 152
Gestapo, Japanese, 90
Goa, 20, 28, 31
God-Sent Troops, 90
Goto Islands, 70
Government, Japanese, 2; educational

234; apostolate of, 214, 215, 233, 234; defense against communism, 213

K., MAGDALENA, 117, 125
Kaempfer, 65
Kagoshima, 17, 18, 21, 23, 39
Kamakura period, 8
Kami, 4; allure of, 7; identification with Buddhist divinities, 7; numerousness of, 30, 97; significance of term, 96; unlike true God, 117
Kanagawa, 189; treaty of, 67
Karafuto, 199
Karasaki, 187
Kaschmitter, Rev. William, M.M., 167
Keller, Rev. James G., M.M., 228
Kempeitai, 90
Kido, Koin, 203
Kimmei, Emperor, 6
Ko, Augustine, 60, 62
Kobe, 43, 71, 108, 126, 127, 132, 135, 147, 179, 180
Kobo Daishi, 7
Koiso, Premier, 1
Konoye, Prince, 99
Korea, 6, 30, 35, 78, 145, 146, 211; annexation of by Japan, 79; Communists smuggled into Yamaguchi from, 211; cultural extirpation in, 125; Japan's relation with, 78
Kusatsu, 187
Kyoto, 12, 24-28, 34, 37, 42, 118, 129, 182-184, 186, 232-233
Kyushu, 33, 34, 53, 62, 70, 175

LABOR MOVEMENT, captured by Communists, 207
Lake Biwa, 186, 11, 37
Land of Morning Calm, 186
Lara, 192
Lawrence, Brother, S.J., 27, 28, 35
Lèse-majesté, 95, 98
Leterdu, Father, 62
Liaotung Peninsula, retrocession of, 78, 79; awarded to Japan, 78
Liberals, Japanese, 163; target of jingoes, 90
Literature, anti-Christian, 166; Catholic social, 192; communistic, 208; dearth of anti-communistic, 208; need of, 213
Living standards, 136, 159
Lord of Heaven, 16, 28, 55, 56, 118
Lourenço Marques, 151-153

Loyalty, in Shinto, 5
Loyalty, quasi-religious, 10
Loyola see Ignatius Loyola, St.
Ludovico, 44
Lukouchiao Bridge, 92

M., DOCTOR, 137, 138
McKillop, Rev. Michael J., M.M., 183
MacArthur, General Douglas, 96, 159, 202, 203
Macao, 48
Mackesy, Rev. William M., M.M., 187
Madagascar, 151
Makino, Count, 90
Malacca, 19, 25
Malaya, 151
Malnutrition, 178, 194
Manchuria, 89, 145, 146, 159, 179
Manchurian Incident, 88, 91
Marella, Archbishop Paul, 145
Marriage, 178, 179
Martyrdom of *Père* Bousquet, 181
Martyrs, Japanese, 49, 63, 69, 175; number of, 52; Twenty-Six Martyrs, 43, 44, 49-51
Marx, Karl, 217, 218, 229
Maryknoll, 182, 233; house of study, 187
Maryknoll Missioners, 38, 145, 149, 154, 182, 183, 227, 228, 232-234; internment of, 108-116, 122, 129
Maryknoll Sisters, 149, 227
Mass, after two centuries, 61; in concentration camp, 131, 132; memorial in tea ceremony, 42; on Oshima, 174, 175
Materialism, 76, 77, 171; *left-wing*, 165; of communism, 219; of Japanese economists, 171; of Japanese sociologists, 171; of natural scientists, 171
Meiji, Emperor, 96; Constitution of, 76
Mentality, Japanese, not philosophical, 96; psychological blind-spot, 123
Merfeld, Rev. Arthur, M.M., 109
Methodists, 72
Mie Prefecture, 188
Mikado, 25, 182
Miki, St. Paul, *see* Paul Miki, St.
Militarism, 139, 140, 203; in Karafuto, 200
Militarists, 157; Sat-Cho group of, 85
Military, 176, 205; advocate of Emperor's divinity, 11; agricultural re-